T0356835

TOUGH

AS A

MOTHER

TOUGH

— *AS A* —

MOTHER

Women in Sports, Working Moms, and the
Shared Traits That Empower Us All

JENN HILDRETH AND AIMEE LEONE

TRIUMPH
BOOKS

Library of Congress Cataloging-in-Publication Data

Names: Hildreth, Jenn, author. | Leone, Aimee, author.
Title: Tough as a…mother: women in sports, working moms, and the shared traits that empower us all / Jenn Hildreth and Aimee Leone.
Other titles: Women in sports, working moms, and the shared traits that empower us all
Description: Chicago, Illinois: Triumph Books, [2025] | Includes bibliographical references.
Identifiers: LCCN 2024046667 | ISBN 9781637277201 (cloth)
Subjects: LCSH: Women athletes—United States—Biography. | Working mothers—United States—Biography. | Work and family—United States.
Classification: LCC GV697.A1 H535 2025 | DDC 796.092/520973—dc23/eng/20241119
LC record available at https://lccn.loc.gov/2024046667

This book is available in quantity at special discounts for your group or organization. For further information, contact:

Triumph Books LLC
814 North Franklin Street
Chicago, Illinois 60610
(312) 337-0747
www.triumphbooks.com

Printed in U.S.A.
ISBN: 978-1-63727-720-1
Photos: Courtesy of interview subjects unless otherwise indicated.

To our own families...

And to all you mamas out there

just trying to keep it all together...

This is for you

Cast of Characters

Debbie Antonelli	College Basketball Analyst
Courtney Banghart	Head Coach, University of North Carolina Women's Basketball
Joscelyn Shumate Bourne	Director of Rehabilitation, Angel City FC
Andrea Brimmer	CMO, Ally Financial
Mary Carillo	Hall of Fame Broadcaster/Professional Tennis Player
Adia Barnes Coppa	Head Coach, University of Arizona Women's Basketball
Susan Saint James Ebersol	Actress, Activist
Jamie Erdahl	Sports Host, Anchor, Reporter
Heather Mitts Feeley	Olympic Gold Medalist—Soccer/Broadcaster
Lisa Milner Goldberg	Vice President of Public Relations, Angel City FC
Tiffany Greene	Play-by-Play Announcer
Andrea Kremer	Hall of Fame Broadcaster
Danette Leighton	CEO, Women's Sports Foundation
Alex Mallen	Senior Director of Corporate Partnerships, Angel City FC
Angela Hucles Mangano	Olympic Gold Medalist—Soccer
Cheyna Matthews	Professional Soccer Player/Jamaican National Team
Sascha Mayer	Co-Founder and Chief Experience Officer, Mamava
Pamela McGee	Olympic Gold Medalist/Women's Basketball Hall of Famer
Jessica Mendoza	Olympic Gold Medalist—Softball/Broadcaster
Alysia Montaño	Olympic Bronze Medalist—Track and Field
Alex Morgan	Olympic Gold Medalist—Soccer
Alana Jane Nichols	Paralympic Gold Medalist—Wheelchair Basketball and Skiing
Hilary and Whitney Phelps	Swimmers, Sisters of Michael Phelps
Susie Piotrkowski	Vice President of Women's Sports Programming and espnW, ESPN
Rebecca Quin (aka Becky Lynch)	WWE Superstar, Champion
Christie Pearce Rampone	Olympic Gold Medalist—Soccer/Broadcaster
Laura Rutledge	Sports Host, Anchor, Reporter
Hannah Storm	Award-Winning Journalist, Producer, Director
Kate Torgersen	Founder and CEO, Milk Stork
Dara Torres	Olympic Gold Medalist—Swimming/Broadcaster
Aliphine Tuliamuk	U.S. Track and Field Olympian
Julie Uhrman	Co-Founder and President, Angel City FC
Aly Wagner	Olympic Gold Medalist—Soccer/Co-Founder, Bay FC Broadcaster
Allison Williams	Sideline Reporter
Katie Witham	Sideline Reporter
Brooke Wyckoff	Head Coach, Florida State University Women's Basketball

Contents

Foreword

I always tell my soccer teammates, "You're stuck with me for life." Whether it's my teammates from Stanford, the U.S. national team, or even my broadcasting teammates now in this part of my life, I'm always going to be calling you, bugging you, and checking in. Jenn and I called eight NCAA women's soccer championships together for ESPN, and Aimee and I first met when I covered my first Olympic Games in 2006. When they told me about this book and shared their vision for supporting and empowering working moms, I said, "Hell *yes*."

Because we all need this. You may not know it yet or you may know it all too well by now, but we absolutely all need this. We need this team of Tough Mothers to support us because being a working mom, like being an elite athlete, is fucking hard. (I should have warned you: I do like to swear.) I wish I had something much more eloquent to say than that, but it's just so damn hard at times. You can't sweep the hard under the rug and pretend it's not there. You have to just embrace it, show it, and know that it's okay to be tired, to look like shit, to say that you didn't sleep last night, and that you need help.

For a long time, we as women couldn't talk about the struggle because we thought it would make us look weak or vulnerable. That facade has cracked, and I think it's time we shatter it with the kind of stories you're about to read in this book. You're not going to be less because you have kids and a family and are willing to show that side of yourself. Just do you…be real, human, authentic, struggling at times, fabulous at other times, and sometimes tired as hell. It is what makes you gloriously *you*. So embrace that and know others will as well.

You shift mindsets by sharing. Look at the U.S. national team, going back to Joy Fawcett, who played with me on the first ever World Cup team and was one of the first to have kids while playing. She was like, "Why do I have to retire? I can pop out a baby and come back. Why not?" And we thought, *No, that's impossible!* But she did just that, and people suddenly *knew*. They knew that being a mom and an athlete were not mutually exclusive. And, no surprise here, but then you had other women on the U.S. team having kids like Carla Overbeck, Christie Pearce Rampone, Shannon Boxx, Alex Morgan, Crystal Dunn, and on down the line. You have these women, who realized by seeing someone else doing it and sharing their experiences, that it's all doable. There is absolutely power to that. It's courage. And courage is contagious.

And then there's the Mom Guilt…ugh…the Mom Guilt is real! I will never forget the time that I was traveling, and my mom was watching my daughter, Izzy. At the time Izzy was about three or four years old, and my mom told me, "Oh, Izzy was playing in the backyard and she looked up and saw an airplane. She pointed at the plane and said, 'Mama.'"

When my mom told me that story, my heart dropped to the floor. My child associated an airplane flying away with Mama? Horrified, I relayed that story to another mom I worked with who laughed and said, "Your child is going to be *just fine*. Mom works, yes. Mom is on a plane at times, yes. But these times are harder on us as moms than the kids. They won't remember pointing to that plane. They will remember a strong, working mom who balanced a lot of things for the family. And they will grow up to be fully functioning adults."

I hope she is right. (Mine are still teenagers, but so far, so good.) As I tell my kids, in my job as a broadcaster, I have to travel. I've covered eight Olympics and nine World Cups, many European Championships, Little League World Series, and Special Olympics World Games. Those certainly aren't happening in my backyard. So although that is challenging, I also think it's so powerful for our kids to see Mom busting her hump.

And, lastly, if I can offer one bit of advice, find your teammates. Tell them they are stuck with you for life. Help each other, support each other, show them grace and love when needed. Pick them up when needed. Kick them in the booty as needed (as my friend did by telling me to calm down and that Izzy will not forever associate her mom with Southwest Airlines). Most importantly, share the struggle so that we know we are not alone. As history has shown with women organizing and gathering throughout the centuries, that is when we are at our most powerful and most effective. It takes a village, party people. Lean into your dope village, mamas, like the one Jenn and Aimee are building for you here. That's the real gift of motherhood.

—*Julie Foudy*

Introduction

To all our mamas out there, let us make this very clear—this is for you. This is about you. You working moms, or about-to-be working moms, who are wondering how you're going to manage the challenges of having it all, we've got you. Because just like the elite athletes and other women you're about to hear from, including Olympic gold medalists like Dara Torres, Pamela McGee, and Alex Morgan; trailblazing broadcasters like Hannah Storm, Mary Carillo, and Andrea Kremer; and bad-ass sports businesswomen like Ally CMO Andrea Brimmer and Angel City co-founder Julie Uhrman; you, too, have everything that you need to succeed.

There are these core traits—these "Tough Mother Tenets" as we like to call them—that really do run through us all. Sacrifice, humility, resilience, moxie—come on, doesn't that sound like you? When you're slapping together a meal while pumping breast milk while keeping an eye on a toddler while (mostly) paying attention to the Zoom call you've got going in the background, you are multitasking just like an elite athlete. Just maybe in a slightly less athletic fashion.

And it doesn't matter if you've never kicked a ball, run a lap, or even watched sports on television. You're a mother; toughness comes with the territory! Now, this is about where our children would roll their eyes and tell us to stop giving them a pep talk. But hang with us. As women who have lived the working mom life and experienced the athlete life through our careers in sports television, we want to share with you the stories that surprised us, inspired us, and opened our eyes to the shared journey that we are all on together. We, Jenn and Aimee, are like the links in this friendship bracelet. Our goal is to tie all of us—our Tough Mothers in this book and you Tough Mothers reading it—together.

We have divided the book into nine parts, one for each Tough Mother Tenet (and for each month of pregnancy). Coincidence? We think not. Within every part, each of our Tough Mothers has a story to share with you in their own words. We tried to place these stories where we thought they fit best, but the reality is that all of us working moms are multifaceted, so you will no doubt see several other tenets running through each of the chapters. And we hope you also see yourself and your own Tough Mother Tenets within these pages. We know all families and stories of motherhood look different. So whether you're a single mom, a mother of multiples, or a parent of a child with disabilities; whether you breastfed or bottle fed; our sisterhood has you covered.

Who knew that the inspiration we needed when we were struggling as working moms was actually all around us in sports? Certainly not us because we straggled on through our struggles, many times feeling isolated and alone. Now we want to share our epiphanies with you.

One message that you will continue to see on these pages—and that you need to remember to look out for in your own lives—is that you are *not* alone. When you're pumping in a bathroom stall, explaining to your child that you can't make it to their school concert, crying in your shower, or feeling sick from the crippling fear that you cannot do it all as a working mom, we are here to remind you that *yes*, yes, you can. But as you'll hear throughout this book, this journey of working motherhood is hard, and no one knows it quite like the women who are going through it themselves.

That starts with speaking the truth and exposing the struggle. And that's what you'll hear as our Tough Mothers pull back the proverbial curtain to expose the grit behind the glamour, the flaws behind the muscle flex, the beast…well, we could go on, but then we'd just be hitting you with too many cringey sports puns. And that's not what this book is about. Our goal is to give you the courage to keep going and the support that we wish we could have had when our kids were younger. We know firsthand that going back to work and leaving your little or not-so-little ones is hard, and maybe that's one of the reasons more moms are leaving the workplace these days.

But having—and keeping—women in the workplace is vital. Come on, you know everybody needs a little more of that girl power in their world, right? And, according to *Forbes* magazine, businesses with women included in senior leadership actually perform better (duh). So let's do this thing. And let's know that we're doing it together. By having honest conversations and feeling the power of this sisterhood, you will realize that we *all* struggle. Being a working mom, we discovered, is one of the great equalizers in life. It doesn't matter who you are or how many resources you have access to. In the end we are all just moms trying to keep it all together.

And those bad-ass, kick-ass traits we mentioned? Our Tough Mothers are going to empower you to uncover and embrace them so that you're better equipped to handle the tough moments that come in your own life. Because when you're in the thick of mom life, especially if you're trying to balance it with work life (and who knows, maybe even a love life from time to time), it's only natural to feel like you're the only one who feels lost in the struggle. Consider us—and the women in this book who will both take your breath away and breathe life into your world—your sisters in arms. We've got bite-sized bits of information and inspiration from close to 40 fucking fabulous women that are here for you to snack on whenever you can find a few minutes for yourself. And we are here to guide you through all of it.

As you flip through the pages, remember these mamas are sharing some insight into what's worked for *them*. But none of us claim to have the road map to success. Our book is not a how-to parenting guide; it's how you, too, can get it done. No one knows your situation better than you do, so please remember to be kind to yourself as you make mistakes and figure it all out. We know your time is precious and we are so grateful that you're choosing to join our sisterhood and share these moments with us. It's worth it, we promise.

XOXO,

Jenn Hildreth, Tough Mother since 2007
Aimee Leone, Tough Mother since 1992

PART I

ADAPTABILITY

—AIMEE

There's something about being adaptable that's just second nature to women. We've had to adapt over the years as culture evolved, as family structure changed, as our roles and demands within the workplace grew...and more. But as intuitive as it may seem, here's one thing you need to remember: it isn't always easy. There's so much we can learn from how the four inspiring Tough Mothers in this section have adapted with each new chapter and challenge in their lives, so it's kind of fitting that it's our first tenet.

NBC broadcaster Mary Carillo always knew she wanted it all. And with the confidence of an athlete and her signature curiosity, she created her own amazing story. You'll learn how former U.S. Soccer captain Christie Pearce Rampone pushed so hard to get back to the national team after giving birth that her body nearly shut down. For the first time in Christie's life, she had to slow down and take care of herself and—perhaps most importantly—learn not to consider any of that a failure. ESPN anchor Hannah Storm made some very intentional career moves as she anticipated the changing needs of her family and she's now committed to sharing her experiences to support women in the thick of juggling both family and career. And Aly Wagner—who in the middle of her not-so-free-time between being a broadcaster, a mom of four, a businesswoman, and a wife— decided to help launch a new soccer club, Bay FC.

I'm a child of the 1960s and was born into the women's liberation movement. It was a really cool time to grow up, especially as a young girl. You could feel that change was in the air, but it was a little bit divisive and a whole lot confusing. My dad was a cartoonist, and my mother stayed at home until I was in middle school. She started working in a local department store and quickly became a talented make-up artist. My father was a big supporter of her going back to work and he had always encouraged her professional growth—even if it meant that our apartment wasn't clean and that he often had to make dinner himself. That may not sound like a big deal now, but back then it was pretty unconventional. Having two working parents wasn't very common, and as a family, we just had to adapt. Sometimes no one was there when we kids got home from school. We grabbed takeout for dinner if everyone was tapped out by then, and I learned to be independent at a very young age. But in spite of the inconvenience, my father supported my mom's decision to go back to work.

And he always encouraged me in that same way. I can't recall a time when I wasn't preparing for a career. I mean, after all, wasn't that the point of those women's marches I grew up attending? I remember going to work with my dad when I was young so I could see what a career actually looked like. This was way before Take-Your-Child-To-Work Day was a thing! On the train into the city and again while sitting in my dad's office on 42nd Street, I couldn't help but notice that there were very few women. But once I watched an episode of *The Mary Tyler Moore Show* in the early 1970s and saw what it looked like to be a young professional woman, I immediately knew that's what I wanted. So, I sought those women out. I zeroed in to see how they dressed, how they carried themselves, and how they interacted with all the men around them. As I got to know some of the women who worked with my dad, I realized that only a few of the successful ones were married, and even fewer were moms. Did women's lib mean that they had to make a choice between family and career? I was confused...I knew I wanted a career and, while I was too young to think seriously about having a family, I knew it was also something I wanted at some point. Was that even possible?

My adultish daughter Claire doesn't fully understand what it was like for a young woman at that time. It seemed we had gained more options in life, sure, but it didn't seem like any of the basic responsibilities of taking care of our family had changed. So I showed her a perfume commercial from the late 1970s that summed it up, and she was horrified. The lyrics went something like this: "I can put the wash on the line, feed the kids, get dressed, pass out the kisses, and get to work by five of nine. 'Cause I'm a woman! I can bring home the bacon, fry it up in a pan. And never, never, never let you forget you're a man. 'Cause I'm a woman."

It's definitely worth the quick Google search to watch it. For me that commercial set this completely unrealistic expectation of what a working mom was supposed to be...and it still haunts me to this day. When I was home after having my first child, my son Jay, I was committed to doing it all. I remember one day when he was a few weeks old and I felt like I had mastered the basics (diapers, breast-feeding, bottle feeding, more diapers, and the dreaded cutting of the nails). Then I was determined to strap him into the BabyBjörn and vacuum the whole house. When he napped in his crib, I did laundry and even cleaned bathrooms. And when my husband Wayne got home from work, I had dinner waiting. I had done it! 'Cause I'm a woman...just like in the commercial, right? OMG, what was I doing? I recently listened to a TED Talk by the brilliant Brené Brown that made me understand my dilemma a little more clearly. She dug in on the shame that women feel from these unrealistic expectations and she referenced the negative impact of that very same commercial. So, it wasn't just me! Sure, that day at home with my newborn, I was able to do it all, but there's no way that was going to be sustainable. The messaging I took from that commercial, well... it's about being everything for everyone else and sacrificing who we are for ourselves.

That led to my next level of adaptation. I didn't want to just have it all, I wanted to enjoy it all...well, at least some of it. Life as a working mom doesn't have to be an endurance test. If I could figure out how to adapt, I had no doubt that the other people in my life would figure it out, too. Wayne and I built a support network—we found a great babysitter, had someone come to help with things around the house, and I joined the neighborhood "stroller brigade," pushing my son around with other young moms and their babies as we shared helpful tips and created a space to be pretty vulnerable about the challenges we were facing. Of course, just when Wayne and I began to adapt to this new normal, something would change—going back to work, traveling, having a second kid, etc.—and it was like, *"Here we go again!"*

That was the start of an incredible journey of working motherhood. Trust me: the road has been bumpy at times, really bumpy. And it looks way different than I thought it would. But to continue along this road analogy, it's a windy one, and you never know what's around the bend. For me it's been about embracing the uncertainty, trying my best, realizing when I needed to adjust, and forgiving myself when I might have missed something. So, as you hear from our first four tough mothers, we hope you find some inspiration for adaptation, some words of wisdom...and maybe even some laughs along the way.

1
MARY CARILLO

Amongst all of the other titles and accolades that Mary Carillo has accumulated throughout the years, storyteller is at the heart of them all. She grew up in Queens, New York, playing tennis alongside John McEnroe, eventually winning a French Open doubles title with him in 1977. After a brief professional playing career, Carillo turned to television, where she has become one of the most well-known and well-loved voices not only in tennis, but also across multiple sports. She has covered 16 Olympics, won an Emmy Award and two Peabody Awards for journalism, is a member of the Sports Broadcasting Hall of Fame, and was a contributor for HBO's renowned documentary series, Real Sports. *She has also written three books, given commencement speeches, produced viral rants about badminton (worth a quick search on YouTube), and raised two children. All with a compassion, drive, and wit that is distinctly, unapologetically, hers.*

I don't know, I think I was a bad ass right from the start. I knew I was getting paid less than other commentators. So let's start there. That's already annoying. There was more than one time that I thought, *I'm better than* this *guy.* When I started out, maybe there was a woman in graphics in the production truck or something. Maybe. I used to be the only chick pretty much. And for a long time, I only did women's tennis because how could I *possibly* call men's tennis, right? It took a long time for me to just get out of strictly covering women's tennis. So that in and of itself was a big deal. And then you want to be able to do everything. You want to be able to do play by play, not just color analysis. You want to be able to do studio stuff, features, interviews, and it wasn't easy. But I don't ever remember pulling back. If anything, I leaned into those guys and said, 'I can do that.' I'm pushy. I'm annoying. That's just me. I never wore dresses. I always wore sneakers. I never tried to doll it up." [Authors' note: To drive this home, Mary stands up and shows off her Bluey T-shirt, the cartoon dog who apparently is a big hit with her grandchildren. She lets out one of those signature Carillo cackles that manifest the pure joy with which Mary does…well… everything.]

"So I didn't go there because I knew that would have been so insincere and disingenuous and false. Then I would have judged myself against other women, and who the hell wants to do that? My whole attitude was: I can do this. And if I can't, I know someone will tap me on my shoulder and tell me to go away. But I know I can do it!

"When my ex and I decided to have kids, it was a big deal because I was just kind of starting to get work away from tennis and doing other sports. But I also knew that I wanted to be a parent. I really wanted to be a mom. There came a time in 1996 when ESPN was getting more tennis, they were wanting me to do more and more stuff, but the kids were little. I didn't want to miss out. I just knew I needed to be home more. So I left ESPN and went to HBO. I left ESPN twice, actually. I'm an idiot! And I mean, this could have gone sideways so easily.

"But Billie Jean King was such a help to me, such a mentor. She had told HBO they should hire me for Wimbledon. She pushed for me to be a consultant on this documentary HBO Sports was doing on the history of women's sports called *Dare to Compete*. And instead of sitting quietly at the table at our first meeting, I'm there like, 'Here's who else we should interview, and we should do this and that and blah blah blah.' Like an idiot! By the end of the project,

I was a co-writer on the doc with the late, great Frank Deford, and it won a Peabody.

"Point being: my decision, which was so stupid, to leave ESPN ended up being this great move. I was at *Real Sports* with HBO for 27 years. And the whole genesis of that decision was to be there more for my kids.

"When you are trying to figure out your work and your love life and your family, when you are juggling all these balls, just remember that some of them are made of glass. Some of the balls don't bounce. So keep that in mind. Don't drop the ones that are made of glass. And I've made 547,000 errors in my life. But even when I got a divorce—my ex Bill and I—I don't think we ever dropped the ball on our kids. When I think back on my working life, I think about how many things I did—for myself, surely; I'm not terribly ambitious, but I'm curious—but I also made decisions for my kids.

"I would make these calendars when they were little with a big red crayon. And I'd show the days that I'd be gone. I'd make the boxes. The first boxes would be small, and then they'd get bigger and bigger, and on the last day, there'd be a big red X through the biggest box just so they could have a sense of time. *This is what the deal is: I'm still going to be gone, but everything's cool!* I never really found it hard navigating that. My mom, though, she didn't really understand. When she got married to my dad—and they've been married now for 70 years—she quit working. It was always her dream to be a wife and a mother, so she felt sorry for women who had to work. So it was kind of interesting growing up with my traditional mother who was concerned that I was spending a lot of time away from my kids. And my ex, Bill, was a great husband, great father, and we had an unbelievable nanny. But I can't tell you how many times when I left for a work trip that my mother would say to me, 'And then you'll be home, right?' Yeah, Ma, then I'll be home. But I also want to be away, and that's okay!

"Once you get it in your head that you want to be good at something, you go there and you commit. Determination. I think of motherhood in much the same way. It's a marathon. And you have to know that it is. But I prefer to compare parenting to tennis. But tennis is played on grass, clay, indoors, outdoors, hard courts. You better be flexible. You better acknowledge that the sun is in my eyes every time I serve on this side. It's windy, it's cold, it's hot. You better be prepared to play a long match. You have to be fit in every way, physically, mentally, emotionally. Everything counts. My poor kids have heard this so many times—but the little things are the big things.

"As soon as you become a parent, you become a coach. This is your job. And your job is to make yourself obsolete. And you have to be okay with that idea. I want to give you every single thing you need to know so you will grow up one day and be a fully formed adult. And you don't need me anymore because you can trust yourself. You know how to solve problems. Coaching, to me, is such an art, and that's what parenting is: figuring out your kid. Figuring out how to make them the best Earthling you can make them. And then getting out of their way.

"My two kids are good athletes, and that is such a blessing for somebody like me. They wanted to be outside running around. They wanted to fall asleep in the car because they'd sweated out their whole day, their juice boxes dangling from their lips. If I had kids that didn't understand the beat of an athletic heart, who didn't understand how hard you have to work to get good at something, it would have been hard for me."

Mary used a lot of lessons from sports with her kids growing up and taught them how to pay attention to the small details and work their butts off even when it was hard, but I think she—and all of us—can instill the beat of the athletic heart into all of our children, athletes or not. I tried my darndest to get my girls into sports because, well, I loved being an athlete but also because I knew how good it was for them. I know what sports can teach you— self-confidence, work ethic, teamwork, discipline, etc.—and I wanted those lessons desperately for my two girls. But they had to want it, too. And while my oldest daughter, Ashley, did choose a sport—figure skating—it was very different from the sports that I grew up playing. Her lessons were different. Her experiences were different. And the cost—holy crap!—that was certainly different. But I believe the baseline that I was hoping sports would instill was still the same. My teenager gets herself up four mornings a week and drives herself (hallelujah for that!) to 6:00 and 7:00 AM practices before a full day of school. That is dedication. My youngest, Maddie, is a middle schooler toying with softball. She loves her bat, paints her cheeks, and picks funny songs for when she walks up to the plate, but I'm not sure she loves the sport. I don't know if she'll stick with it or if she'll choose to put in the dedication that staying in sports requires. But I do know that this kid will work hard at whatever she does. So I interject this here because I genuinely believe that Mary would have done the same if her kids had not been athletes; she would have found another way to impart the lessons that were so important to her.

—J.H.

"My son, Anthony, tells this story. He was a real caveman tennis player, just wanted to hit everything hard. He remembers me taking him out on the court and he just wanted to hit big from one spot. He said I stopped and said to him, 'Anthony, if I'm working harder than you are, something's wrong.' He remembers! He tells that story; I don't even remember! You never know what's gonna stick with kids. It's important to remember that, too.

"My daughter was an intern with me at the 2012 Olympics in London. It was great. We got to hang together for a month. I worked 6:00 PM to 6:00 AM; that was my shift, and she was with me the whole time. And when it was still dark, we'd walk back together to the hotel. She still talks about it. It was just one of the all-time best experiences together because she got to see who I work with and what it's like. She got to see the engine room of it all. And she realized why I like working so much. At that Olympics I happened to score two tickets for my son and his girlfriend to the gold medal women's beach volleyball game. It was August 8, my son's birthday, and he calls me. There's so much noise, and he's saying, 'Mom, I don't even know if you can hear me, but this is the greatest birthday present of all time!' That was I think the only Olympics that they came to, but they came to a lot of tennis. I snuck Anthony and seven of his friends into Wimbledon one year, still one of the highlights of his life. They hid behind a van in the parking lot.

"I think they liked getting to know what I did and why I did it. They learned how to tell a good story. And my father was an art director. My brother is a novelist. My sister, Gina, acted when she was younger. My son is an actor. We all seem to think we have stories to tell."

2
CHRISTIE PEARCE RAMPONE

*Christie Pearce Rampone is a U.S. Soccer Hall of Famer, four-time Olympian, and three-time Olympic gold medalist. She also played in five FIFA Women's World Cups, winning two of them, including the historic 1999 title at the Rose Bowl in Los Angeles. She wrote her own book—*Be All In: Raising Kids for Success in Sports and Life, *became a television analyst for FOX Sports, and coached her daughters, Rylie and Reece, who you will hear from at the end of this chapter. Although it's become much more common to see moms like Alex Morgan and Crystal Dunn come back to play for the U.S. national team after having children, Rampone was one of the first OG Soccer Moms. In fact, she was just the fifth woman to do it and she did it not once...but twice. It was all part of an incredible career that was notable both for its excellence and its longevity. She played into her 40s—which is rare for a professional soccer player—and amassed more than 300 appearances for the national team, amongst the most for any male or female in the world.*

"Competing and playing was a joy for me. The stress of just getting to the job was the hard part. We didn't even always have seats together on the plane when I traveled with my kids. I would always wonder and stress out about if what I was doing was going to affect them long term. I'd hear other friends talk about having kids and say, 'They're in bed by 7:00.' And it's like my kids have never been on a schedule—ever!

"As they got older, I'd get a lot of: 'Isn't it time to give it up? Isn't it time that you're home with your kids?' A lot of people assume that once you choose to be a mom, you have to give up your career. But

I certainly didn't think that way. And I believed that I was building a foundation for our family. My oldest, Rylie, really respects it a lot now and she wants to follow in my footsteps of being a working mom. But it was scary, I will admit. When people call you selfish, you're like, *Wait, what? No, I'm doing this for all of us.* That's why I brought my kids on the road. I wanted them to see the world and to be around their mom as much as possible. I had faith that in the end they'd get it. They'd understand the reason why Mom put so much time into staying fit and to playing into her 40s.

"They've seen me go through a lot. And even when they were younger, they learned how to adapt and adjust to just about any circumstance. Rylie was born in September of 2005, and the next big tournament for the U.S. was scheduled around four months later. I worked hard to get myself ready to play, and baby Rylie and I were both on the plane—for a 14-hour flight—when we headed to China for the tournament. We made it through the flight, but when we got to the hotel, there was nothing for Rylie. No crib. Nothing. Well, we were exhausted, and I had to figure something out, so I literally pulled a drawer out of a dresser, padded it with some blankets, and put her in there right next to me in the bed. Of course, you don't sleep that way! Here I am, a working mom on the road, and my child has nowhere to sleep. I'm just making do, taking deep breaths. But at that point you question, *Am I doing the right thing?* As a female I always wanted to show that I was strong. I wanted to prove to my daughters—and to everyone else—that I could live out my dream and have a career as well as be a mom. But moments like this—they test you in every possible way.

"I was allowed to have a nanny on trips, but what I don't think people realize is that it was usually a sibling of a player or a mother, someone I'd pick that would want to experience traveling with their friend or daughter. So I didn't expect anything at night from them. I did everything. Even when I did get some sleep, I was still getting up every three hours to breastfeed. When I walked out of my room the next morning, though, no one knew—except maybe for the bags under my eyes!

"I was about six months in with Rylie when something strange started happening. I was talking gibberish, and my body just felt like it was giving up on me. I thought I was having a stroke. After training I went to get some tests done. They showed all the signs of a stroke yet also indicated that I'd never actually had one. Between the dryer weather out in California where I was for camp and all the travel that I'd been doing—not to mention the breastfeeding—I knew I wasn't hydrating enough. But I had no idea of just how bad of shape I was in. At that point I had to reevaluate. *Was I taking care of myself?* I was trying to grind through, do everything that I thought was right as a working mother. *But what about me?* Once again, it got me wondering: *Could I really do both? Be on this world-class team and be a mom? Was it actually possible?* At least for the time being, I realized that I had to shift my focus to myself—*my* nutrition, *my* health, *my* well-being. It can't just be go-go-go all the time. You've got to take that deep breath and reevaluate. From that point on, once I started taking better care of myself, things started to click.

That reminds me of the pre-flight safety video where they tell you to put your mask on first before helping young children. My friends and I have talked about how counterintuitive that is because as moms we're so hardwired to help our kids first. I remember when I was pregnant with my second child, Claire. I spent just about every non-working non-commuting moment taking care of my three-and-a-half-year-old son Jay and I completely neglected myself. My doctor told me that if I didn't make serious changes—eat better, sleep, and reduce stress—that he would have to put me on bed rest. As hard

"When I had my second daughter, Reece, I felt like it was really important for me to be present for my club team, Sky Blue FC. I had been able to live out my dream and play at the highest level and I wanted the younger players on my team—and the players coming after them—to have the same opportunities even if that meant at times doing the team laundry. I would literally scrub and clean the team uniforms. There didn't seem to be anyone else doing it, so I just did it myself—with a toddler and a newborn!

"I'll never forget one time we traveled out to California for a game. The locker room had no air conditioning, and it was hot. Reece never did like the heat and she was just bawling. I had a nanny helping me out on this trip, and she felt awful because she couldn't do anything to calm Reece down. I knew she didn't need a diaper change or food, so I needed to do something to help her with the heat. I turned on one of the showers, plopped Reece down under the cool water, and thankfully she quieted right down. The nanny stayed in the locker room with her the entire game. I'm pretty sure no baby books recommend putting your child in a shower for two hours to calm them down, but, hey, as working mothers, we find a way to make it work!

"As my girls got older, I did have to miss a lot. It hurts, and you do feel guilty, but there are ways to get through it. One year I missed Reece's end-of-season soccer celebration. It was one of those things where all the parents came, but I couldn't be there because Rylie had a big varsity game at the same time, and I was the coach. I couldn't be in two places at once. So I had to think outside the box. I made these big fathead face cutouts and had the other moms hold them up. I made Reece a sign with a quote on it and added some candy for her, and she was like, 'Oh my God, this is the best thing ever!'

"There are so many ways to stay connected even when you can't physically be together. And it happens over time. The journey to winning a World Cup or an Olympics doesn't happen overnight. The relationship and bond you build with your teammates takes years, and it's the same thing with your children. It's challenging just being a mom, never mind adding work to it. It's all-encompassing. You're trying to do the best you can, but you can't be perfect. I think sports taught me that. You're going to have bad days. But at the end of the day, you've got to look at the big picture. No one ever said it was going to be easy, but we are tough mothers. I'm a tough mother.

"I have always tried to be the constant in my daughters' lives, no matter what was shifting and changing around us. I think consistency is what kept me playing soccer for so long and what has made me a good mom. And you know what? Looking back now, I wouldn't change anything. I would do it all the same way. My girls are two strong-minded, independent females, and that is no coincidence. They have been raised around strong females. They have been inspired their whole lives."

My mom is amazing. She was able to have two kids and continue to play at the highest level. My mom is very focused and determined, and I know this played a big part in her success. She never made being a mom an excuse. As her daughter I knew I had the best mom in the world. Thank you, Mom, for giving me your tough mentality in school and sports. I now look forward to challenges and see them as opportunities because of you. You have taught me so many things but most importantly to be kind to others and help those in need.

—daughter Reece at age 14

I was able to grow up around some pretty amazing women. I saw the hard work and dedication they put into playing on the best team in the world. I witnessed the good and bad times, travel, pressure, the hours of work put in away from the cameras. My mom and her teammates showed me what it takes to be confident, strong, and independent women. My mom is a Tough Mother because even when playing for the best team in the world she was always my mom first. She has been the most consistent presence in my life. She raised me and my sister pretty much on her own and takes on more than I could handle while always being kind. Thank you, Mom, for being you and not changing because you won three gold medals and two World Cups. You inspire Reece and I every day.

—daughter Rylie at age 19

3
HANNAH STORM

Main photo: AP Images

Hannah Storm is one of those names that's familiar to anyone who watches sports television . She is an anchor on ESPN's flagship show, SportsCenter, *but she has also worked most marquee events such as the NBA Finals, Olympics, Wimbledon, U.S. Open, Super Bowl, New York Marathon, and World Series. Storm was the first play-by-play voice of the WNBA and teamed up with fellow Tough Mother Andrea Kremer on Prime Video to become the first all-female, full-time broadcast team calling NFL games. But as much as Storm loves sports—and she will tell you it is wired into her DNA, which is part of the reason she named her podcast* NBA DNA—*do not try to slap just one label on this woman. Storm is a producer, director, an author, a former mascot, hard rock DJ (that's where she got the moniker "Storm"), former CBS morning show host, a cancer survivor, a mother of three, a wife who recently celebrated her 30th anniversary, a pretty darn good cook, and a master of making her multifaceted career fit into the multi-layered life she wants to lead.*

I chose a career path that I love but that took so much tenacity and positivity. That's what it took to just keep going and moving past so many hurdles. I started my career in the late '80s, and at that time sportscasting was not a viable career option for women. But I knew I wanted to go into broadcasting and I knew I wanted to do sports. My dad was a sports executive, and as a kid, my mom would always put me in two things—art and sports. I did it all—figure skating, softball, soccer, track—I was also, very importantly, our school mascot. That's an important piece of athletic achievement.

"But having that background was a real blessing because it allowed me to move past a lot of bigotry, a lot of questioning of 'Could a woman really do this?' It allowed me to withstand an enormous amount of rejection through the years because I really wanted to do it, and I was pretty stubborn and determined. So to come to the point where you still have that drive and passion for what you do, but you are also a mother and you love being around your children, you're faced with the constant challenge of trying to balance it all. It's been really interesting and evolving for me, and I don't think working motherhood is one size fits all. I think it depends on your kids' ages and your situation. A lot of times we focus on working moms with little kids, but what does it mean to be a working mom of a teenager? A pre-teen? An adult child? Because that dynamic changes through the years.

"When I was with Aimee at NBC, we would go to the Olympics, Wimbledon, the NBA playoffs. My kids were really little at the time. So they didn't have a huge awareness of 'Oh, Mom's not here on the weekend.' They weren't in school. So it was also a lot more flexible if my husband or I wanted to take them with us. I remember taking my oldest daughter to an NBA game in Chicago and I turn around and there she is sitting in the lap of Dr. J [NBA Hall of Famer Julius Erving].

"Once they get into school, it's a completely different ballgame. I was transitioning from NBC and I told my agent, 'I do not want you to look at a weekend job and I don't want you to look at any job that happens at night. Nothing. Don't even look.' Because I wanted to be gone a part of the day that was least impactful to my children. I ended up going to CBS and hosting *The Early Show* for five years. I was gone in the mornings, but I was there for every sporting event, everything after school, weekends, all of it. That ended up being an incredible job for having kids. At ESPN I launched the

Monday through Friday morning *SportsCenter*. So the hours for the
most part were still good. Trips and travel did happen, and that for
me has always been the toughest thing. Going to Wimbledon in
England, it's like a three-week commitment, and I just got to the
point where I didn't feel great. I felt untethered. I was like, *I can't sit
here in England while they're having summer at home.* So I gave up
Wimbledon. That was hard. I basically lost most of the tennis that I
had been working on as a result of that.

Even when you know something is right in your heart, and that it's best for
your family, that doesn't mean it's going to be easy. I felt that when I decided
to leave my job reporting for the Atlanta Braves in 2015. The Braves were
really the first professional sports team that I adopted as my own, and one of
my first jobs was working as a reporter at what was then FOX Sports South.
I started out doing feature reporting for college sports and dreaming about
reporting on some of the bigger properties that our network covered like the
Braves. I wasn't great at advocating for myself, but after working hard for
over a decade, I pushed for more opportunities and I was offered the job. I
loved the feel of being in the ballpark, penciling in my scorecard every game,
and coming up with new and interesting questions to ask the players and
managers.

But here's the thing about Major League Baseball: the season is
looooooooooong (162 games). I never did more than 50 games in a season,
but even that—on top of the college football and basketball sideline reporting and college soccer play by play that I was doing—was still a lot. And
instead of going away for one game and maybe a couple of days at a time,
sometimes I would be gone for eight-to-10 days. Even covering home games
meant that I would leave around lunch time and not return until late at
night. My daughters were so little then; Ashley was in grade school, and
Maddie was just a curly-headed, tutu-wearing toddler. I knew it was too

much. But I also knew that it was something I had worked really hard for and that I enjoyed. In the end, after talking with my husband, my family won out. I know I made the right choice, but it was still hard. Figuring out that balance of how much time away is too much time away, it's a never-ending challenge for working moms.

–J.H.

"We all make choices; sometimes they work out, sometimes they don't, and we have to adjust. But this is the essence of what being a working mother is: always trying, changing the journey along the way, and at some point bringing your children along with you—not physically, but having them understand mentally and emotionally what you're going through and what your thought process is in regards to them and to the family.

"It was always so hard for me when I had to leave. But I think sometimes we torture ourselves unnecessarily. I'd be like, 'Oh, I've gotta go…I don't want to go.' And they're like, 'We're fine!' There are so many factors that go into what happens with your children and how they develop. To have the honestly myopic view that anything negative that may happen only has to do with you and the decisions you make regarding work, that's just not true. That's not accurate. So understand that it's okay for you to not always be there. It's okay to have your partner there or maybe at times have your parents there or someone else in your family and give them those really special memories with your kids. That's kind of cool. When I worked mornings, my husband Dan drove the girls to school every day. They listened to music and bonded over their favorite musicians and they still go to concerts together to this day. There are times when I was having terrible FOMO—which I wish was a word that had always existed because I would have used it for decades—when he would be there at times that I wasn't able to be. But *he* was there. That was the important thing.

"And it's also kind of good for your kids to be flexible, adaptable, and know that Mom's not always going to be there 100 percent of the time to pick up the pieces. They need to learn to be independent. I think overall you want to make sure that your child feels secure, feels loved, and has self-confidence. To me that's the No. 1 thing you can give, especially to a young woman. When my oldest daughter went to college, she said, 'Mom, I'm just so glad you worked. You gave me the license to be ambitious. You showed me what it means to follow your dreams and be passionate about what you do. You showed me that. And I'm going to do the same.' Honestly, when she said that—and she has said subsequent things like that, and I've heard versions of it from my other daughters—it's really…everything.

"A lot of young women have come to me for advice, and what pains me the most is when they feel like they have to hold off having a child or they feel like they can't have a child because of the demands of their work. If you can, flip this around and think about making your work fit into your family life—if you have that luxury—and I know a lot of mothers in this country don't have that luxury. But your job is your job. Your family and your job, they really are not on par. Your family, and your legacy as a mom, is so far ahead of whatever awards are sitting on your shelf when you die or how much money you make. To me, your family, that's your legacy.

"And we as moms need to support other moms or people who are thinking about becoming moms. We need to let them know you're not alone. Especially with social media. I think there's a lot of pressure on young moms now to cultivate a social media following and create this whole other life for people to see. There's a lot of time and energy spent on that, and I think it breeds a whole lot of insecurity because you're looking at other families and other moms, and they look perfect. I think that it has the same effect on older women that it does on teenage girls and younger women, which is incredibly damaging. Holding yourself to a standard that is not realistic, and pretending to always be the perfect mom is a real burden. And it's one that we don't need in our lives. No one is giving out a Best Mom Award at the end of the day. There is no such thing as best mom because every mom is different. So I think sharing, really being honest, and having people understand that they are part of a community and that you're not alone is so important. I hope I have been able to show women that they can go about their careers and not be afraid to try new things, to put themselves out there, to work really hard, and still be able to adapt and love their lives as a mom."

4

ALY WAGNER

Aly Wagner is "the visionary." That's what her business partner and former teammate Danielle Slaton told the Sports Business Journal *when asked about the four women who founded National Women's Soccer League Club, Bay FC. Wagner and Slaton make up two of the Founding Four, along with Leslie Osborne and Brandi Chastain. All four played for the U.S. national team, and all four are mothers. Wagner's vision is part of what led her to become a two-time Olympic gold medal-winning player and one of the top soccer analysts in the United States. She was FOX Sports' lead match analyst for the 2019 and 2023 FIFA Women's World Cups and in 2018 she became the first woman in U.S. English-language television history to call a men's FIFA World Cup match. Next came the founding of a soccer club that Wagner hopes will raise the bar and change the world. She and her husband Adam have triplet boys—Griffin, Daeven, and Lincoln born in 2013—and a daughter, Blake, born in 2015.*

"There's been so much as an athlete that has helped me both as a mom and as a mom in a career. Discipline, organization, structure are all incredibly valuable. A lot of people with one baby, they can get away with naps on the road, food to go, stuff like that. You cannot do that with triplets. You need them all on the same schedule. That gives you a greater understanding of what they need in the moment, and you can predict and adjust to their needs. Because what I've found is that if you don't put them on a schedule, you have no idea of what could be off. As far as making sure that you spend time with them, I feel like I was so much in an assembly line of breastfeeding and doing that I never just held them and got to be with them. I was so much in survival mode. So I would say to try and take advantage of that opportunity because before you know it they're 10 years old, and you'll be wanting those moments back.

"When I first had our triplets, my stepmother-in-law said, 'You've changed, you're so much softer now.' Call it a lack of self-awareness, but I didn't really realize that I didn't come across as soft or nurturing before having kids. I think that definitely shifted me, though. And I think it's finding the right balance. Do I still have to be more nurturing at times and not as hard on my kids? Probably. But I'm a strong believer in boundaries, expectations, communication, and in setting up the right structure for them to grow as individuals. That definitely comes from my background as an athlete. But then the love and the connection and the support is what makes that structure and framework work for them.

"As an athlete you have to be the calm in the storm. You're taught that you need to stay focused on what really matters on the field. I think dealing with uncertainty and chaos and normalizing that and not letting that upset your balance, that's really valuable as a mom. So many times, stuff is swirling around you—you might need to get something done for work, and your kid wants a snack, or you're worried about a fight they had at school—all these things that are swirling and you are in the middle of it. You're never going to be able to anticipate everything, but trying to stay ahead of the needs and the demands that are going to be on you as a mom, that is one piece that sport absolutely taught me. That being said, I wasn't prepared at all for the arrival of our triplets.

"When you get pregnant with triplets, they recommend that you go to a high-risk obstetrician. The doctors will give you data that is pretty daunting about how unlikely it is that all three babies will be healthy. We just tried to trust our instincts and for me to listen to what my body was telling me throughout the pregnancy. All the literature about triplets says that you should put on as much weight as possible, be pretty sedentary, so you can create as healthy an environment as possible for your babies to get big and strong. As an athlete that didn't feel right to me, so I just kept working out—I mean lightly, I wasn't doing anything crazy—and I felt great. And I was just eating what my body was telling me I needed. That was right up until the 28th week. My belly was already so big—it would be a full-term belly for someone else—and I felt like contractions were happening. So we went to the doctor, and they thought it was preterm labor out of nowhere—at 28 weeks! They were able to do something to stave off the contractions. I was in the hospital for a few days, and then they sent me home but put me on bed rest. They said to just lay on my left side because that gets the most blood flow to the babies.

"I stayed on bed rest until Week 33 and then I asked if we could move up the C-section to 34 weeks because I felt like the babies were running out of room. They were in the NICU [neonatal intensive care unit] for 13 days after they were born and then they all came home together, which was pretty cool. Twins and triplets rarely all come home from the NICU on the same day. But I had been so nervous that my babies were not going to make it or be healthy that I didn't really prepare for their arrival; I didn't want to jinx anything. I wish I would have done more research, asked the right questions, and prepared myself for coming home. It was a whirlwind once they were home. We were fortunate enough to have night nannies, which I think is really helpful for the first month, but everyone should do their research there. Get the right people. Do your due diligence before your triplets get home because once they get home it's just chaos. You're basically breastfeeding and sleeping all day.

"Some of the best advice that I could give to parents of multiples is to not always group them together. With our triplets we're lucky that they're so unique. They look different and they have very different personalities. But I think we still forget at times that they are individuals. My kids recently changed schools, and when they went to tour the new school, there were two classes that they could be in at their grade level. One of my sons, Griffin, got in one class, and the other two boys went together in the other. And when they got home, I was asking them about it, how they liked it, things like that, and the first thing Griffin said was, 'Mom, there was finally space for me.' I feel like I'm pretty in tune with my kids, but he's not anyone that I would have imagined feeling that way. He's loquacious, he's confident, and I thought he would be comfortable stepping into the light as a unique individual. Clearly, that was something that maybe he didn't even realize that he wanted or needed to ask for. So it was a very sweet moment but also a good reminder that when you have twins or triplets, grouping them together is inevitable, but you also need to be aware of their own individual identities.

"As for balancing work and family, I would absolutely recommend that you take your kids with you on the road as often as possible. Showing them your work is incredibly important. They get to see the effort that you put into something outside of the family, and I think that's really valuable for them to see strong women who contribute to the world, contribute to the economy. Those are the data points that are actually going to change the stereotype about women and are going to get us to equality faster than any initiatives. It starts with the home and the family.

Some of our moms prefer to keep work and family separate but not Aly. She has that laser focus about her work, yet somehow, she manages to find opportunities to create memories during rare moments of down time on the road. Whether it's celebrating with her family at the launch of Bay FC, touring "down under" on an off day of the Women's World Cup, or riding camels through the desert in Qatar, it's clear that's what works for her. But hey, it's not for everyone. So when the time comes for you to make that decision, you do you.

−A.L.

"Having them around you and by you while you work helps to balance things out. What are we doing in this world if we're not enjoying our family and our life? If I was just working all the time and was focused on my career, that's not as rewarding as being able to share those experiences with my family and having them by my side. And just selfishly as a mom, I want to be with them. If that means them coming with me, then that's the solution. Sometimes you need time away, but for the most part, the more often that you can have your children in your orbit, the better off they'll be and the better off you'll be.

"I don't think I'll see the impact my role has had on my kids until they're a little older and I really see what they noticed and what mattered to them. The one thing they do notice, which is not great, is that they think that I'm famous. I don't want them focused on the wrong thing. Focusing on being famous is not a strategy. Go find something that you love, find something that you're passionate about, and put in the work. If it leads you to fame and popularity, then so be it, but don't make the outcome be your goal. Don't let the fame be the driver. It's just a byproduct of the work.

"This third iteration of my career as a co-founder of Bay FC is really centered around something that hopefully changes the world. I say it's potentially the most meaningful part of my career because if we can stand shoulder to shoulder with the top men's clubs in the world, we can change everything. Not only do we want to provide a place for players to play where they can maximize their skillset on the field, but we also want to make sure that they have the resources to then go into the next phase of their careers once they're done playing. That's the foundation of what we're doing. By setting that standard, there will be so many downstream effects—not just in the United States but globally. Getting respect for women around the world in many countries where it still doesn't exist, that's an important step to driving toward equality and opportunity. It's giving back and creating a new standard, a new normal, for the world.

"I'm home more now in my work with Bay FC, which is a blessing, but my kids will say, 'Mom, why are you always on calls or in meetings? Where are you going? Why are you going into the city?' I can't always pick them up from school now. I can't always take them to school. So it's different. It's fluid, the dynamics of being a mom. Before, I could compartmentalize. When I was focusing on breaking down games as a broadcaster, I'd take my notes and I could turn it off. I knew the cadence and the pace at which I had to dig into all the teams I was going to be covering. We just took a vacation, and I couldn't turn work off. I actually couldn't step away from it. So while it's great to be home and not traveling as much, now my focus is different, but it's almost more consuming because it's 24/7. So that dynamic is really challenging for me just to be able to try to turn it off and set aside the time to be present with my littles. Being a mom is basically prioritizing, figuring out what really matters. Do I need to get this email out or do I need to deal with my daughter that had a bad day at school? And figuring out what is actually the most important thing in the moment. That's a sport skillset, and it's one that is constantly changing and evolving."

PART II
MOXIE

—JENN

Moxie. I love this word. Most definitions include terms like determination and perseverance, and we working moms—along with elite athletes—definitely possess those traits. Pamela McGee, who along with her son JaVale became the first mother/son duo to win Olympic gold medals, is absolutely made of moxie. Keep a notebook handy when you're reading her chapter because she is chock full of witty words to live by. You'll see, too, why Olympic runner Alysia Montaño would make a great president. She has this incredible fighting spirit that not only pushes her to stand up for herself, but also to fight for the rights of all mothers. And my friend Debbie Antonelli is a Hall of Fame broadcaster and an absolute force to be reckoned with when it comes to women's basketball, her family, and advocating for her middle son, Frankie, who was born with Down syndrome.

These women have ignited my own moxie, though I give my mom and dad a lot of credit for that too. My parents, Joe and Sandra Hildreth, are educators, artists, and archers. My mom shot a perfect score of 300 at an indoor archery tournament—when she was massively pregnant...with me. I also got plopped on a horse in Utah for a bowhunting trip at the age of four months. Later as a curly-headed toddler, I proudly hung my favorite toy, Scooter (the bespectacled orange assistant to Kermit on *The Muppet Show*) from a clothes hanger-shaped contraption meant to string up gutted deer. Mine was a childhood of outdoor adventure and ambition. My dad would pull pigtails so tight they made my eyes water before dropping me off at school. Later, when I got home, he would ask me, "Who is the smartest in your class? The prettiest? The fastest?"

Determined and competitive before I even knew the words to define my drive, I always answered with more than a modicum of moxie: "Me." The line between self-confidence and stuck-up-ed-ness is a fine one, especially for girls, but I wouldn't stumble into that minefield until my teens. My mom and dad taught me that I could do anything that I wanted, and for that I am so grateful. I think that belief in yourself and your abilities is a huge building block to making moxie.

Branching out a little further on my family tree, there's a matri-archy on both sides led by grandmothers who each in their own way possessed such strength of character. On my mother's side is my Grandma Jackie or "GG" to my daughters. Recently, my mom discovered a photo of my grandmother from the early 1940s, right around the time that she graduated from high school. She is laying on a towel in the grass on her right side, her right elbow propping her up, and her left arm angled over her head in a rather alluring (for the time) come hither fashion. The grin on her face is part seduc-tress, part cat who ate the canary like she is in on some delicious secret and wouldn't you like to know. In fact, my grandma was actually on a bicycle tour in her home state of Wisconsin. She and a friend went by themselves, staying in hostels at night. My brother and I were both kind of shocked by this news. After all, that seems pretty progressive for a single young woman in the 1940s, doesn't it? My mom agreed that, yes, my grandmother was pretty progressive. Perhaps, she said, even a little rebellious. Jacqueline Marquardt (as my grandmother was known before she got married) also served in the WAAC—the Women's Army Auxiliary Corps, the women's branch of the United States Army—in Washington, D.C., during World War II. "Once she got married and I came along," my mom said, "her adventurous spirit was shut down."

You can feel the sadness in my mother's words. Motherhood, it seems, took my grandmother's moxie. At least for awhile. I think later in life she started to find it again. Grandma Jackie raised her family and collected antiques but also helped start a new Unitarian church in Bowling Green, Kentucky. She began taking psychology classes on Carl Jung in her 50s. She always drove a red car. That rebellious spirit was, thankfully, never completely snuffed out.

On the other side was my dad's mom, my Grandma Willa. She, too, lived in Bowling Green, and we drove from our home in New York to visit our grandmothers and other family members at least twice a year while I was growing up. My youngest daughter, Madison, takes her middle name from my Grandma Willa, whose full maiden name was Willa Gray Wilson. This was the grandmother who spoiled us to death as grandkids. She loved to buy us things and make us treats. (Her candy cane cookies are still a treasured family recipe that we all make around the holidays.) If my dad would get on my brother or me about something, my grandma would be quick to swoop in with a big hug and say, "Bless its heart!"

Spoiling her grandkids was a luxury that Grandma Willa did not have as a mother to her own boys, my dad Joe and my uncle Mike. Their father passed away when my dad was just 10 years old, and my grandma had to fight tooth and nail as a single mom for many years to keep her children clothed and fed. Life was hard, but this is a woman whose backbone was stronger than maybe even she knew. And she certainly had enough smarts to rely upon. Grandma Willa skipped a year in high school and graduated at the top of her class. She also—and this blows my mind—played basketball. I mean, how many girls basketball teams were there in the 1930s? But she showed me the black-and-white team photo. Even into her 70s, my grandmother loved the game. She was a season-ticket holder to both the men's and women's basketball teams at Western

Kentucky University, and I think she probably had a lot to do with my early love for the sport.

My mother is quiet but full of strength and spirit as well, and I'll get more into her incredible influence later in the book. It's safe to say that I have been blessed with a matriarchy of moxie. I know that I needed it, too, both to pursue my career and mother my children. As far as my job, I like to say that I now sit in, as I call it, "the big girl's seat." In the simplest terms, the play-by-play announcer tells you the who and the what of a broadcast while the analyst provides the why and the how. When I got started in sports television, I had never, ever imagined myself in this role. Part of that may have been because I simply didn't see—or hear—women doing play by play very often. Over the last few decades, that has started to change, and I am proud to be one of the female play-by-play voices that is a part of that movement. But that doesn't mean I wasn't scared as hell when I started. And I certainly had to rely on more than a little bit of moxie to carry myself through the doubts both in my mind and on social media. Not everyone, as you can imagine, loves a female voice, especially if you happen to be calling men's sports.

As I was progressing in my career, I also desperately wanted to succeed in my personal life as a wife and as a mother. When my husband, Chris, and I decided to have children—and we always knew that we wanted to—I never once considered staying home to take care of them. This is in no way a slight to those who choose this path; I honor and respect stay-at-home moms and am truly in awe of many of my friends who do such an incredible job excelling in that role. I just knew that it wasn't for me.

My husband has also been a hands-on dad since Day One. He has never shied away from changing diapers or cooking food. In the early days with both girls, he would get up and sit with me while I nursed, sometimes giving our baby a bottle from my previous pumping session. I went back to work and back on the road not long after the birth of both our children, and Chris just handled it. And for that—and many other things—I am so grateful. So are my two daughters, who love their daddy and prefer that he still cooks their meals (another win for me). So while on this journey, let's not forget to thank and appreciate the partners and other people in our lives who help make it all possible as we forge our paths, find our voices, and charge up our moxie.

5
PAMELA McGEE

AP Images

Women's Basketball Hall of Famer Pamela McGee was the first in a lot of things: first WNBA player to have both a son (JaVale, NBA) and daughter (Imani, WNBA) play professional basketball, first-round draft pick of the first-ever WNBA draft, and part of the first mother/son duo to win Olympic gold medals. McGee is quite possibly the Mama Matriarch of the First Family of American professional basketball. But she'll also be the first to tell you that life ain't easy. Not when you're a young African American woman, a single mom, a basketball player with no guiding footsteps to follow, and not when you're at the center of a very public custody battle over your daughter, one that questions your ability to be a good mom because of your career. Though that battle took its toll on both mother and daughter, the two have since found their way back to one another. McGee was taught by her own mother that she was made to be at the top of the food chain. She likes to take inspiration from what she calls "The Constitution of Diane McGee," and Pamela—like her mother, Diane—is proof that there is nothing quite so powerful as a mother's voice.

"Who takes a nine-month old baby into a foreign country where you don't even speak the language? My son wasn't planned. Having a baby was not in the plans that I had for my life at that time. When I look back, if I'm totally honest, I really don't remember a lot of it because it was so hard. But I had this underlying drive to where I felt I had to work twice as hard as everybody else because I had this baby and I wanted to prove that I could do it. It was just: this is what I want to do and this is what I need to do. I told my agent,

'If I can't get a nanny, then that team can't hire me. I need to make sure my son can travel with me.' And because at the time I was an elite athlete, one of the top five in the world, they gave me whatever I wanted. But I did make sacrifices. You cannot have it all. [Authors' note: Hearing that nearly stopped our hearts. After all, aren't we promising you stories of encouragement?]

"As working mothers, we do ourselves a disservice to think we can have it all. And what I mean by that is you have to make some sacrifices. You're going to have to give up something. That's just the reality of life. Sometimes my house wasn't as clean as I wanted it to be. I'd get back from a game and was like, *I'm tired. I'm going to sleep.* So I gave up having a clean kitchen, but I did it so I could get up in the morning and get JaVale ready for his finals.

"I couldn't play in Russia because I had a child. Russia paid the most money, but because I was a mother, I said, 'I can't take my baby there.' I have lost some jobs where they said, 'Your kids are too much of a priority.' And I said, 'Okay, then I need to go find another job.' My philosophy has always been: I can always make money. I know how to make money. But the stuff that I have with my children and what I impart on them, that's where I've tried to make people-first decisions. Children really don't care about a lot of stuff. They do care about your presence.

"I think you set unrealistic goals as an overachiever and a perfectionist. I always tell women, 'Wonder Woman is dead. I'm not trying to be her.' And sometimes we try to be everything. You are not going to be that perfect mom. She does not exist. Now, I will be the best mom that I can be, and if that looks different to you, well, I don't care.

"Sports for me have been a gift. Both my children got scholarships. It allowed me to travel around the world. And I know that I'm different than most women. I just know it because I didn't grow up playing with dolls. I grew up in Flint, Michigan, on the basketball court with all men, saying, 'I got next.' And I wasn't afraid. And so when I navigate the corporate world, I'm never afraid. I say, 'There's money on the table. Let's go get it!' I know a lot of women don't think like that. But as I try to explain to my kids, normal is over-rated. JaVale would always say to me, 'Why can't you just be like all the other moms?' And I'm like, 'All the other moms are not Hall of Famers. You have a Hall of Fame mom!'

"My standard is totally different because I'm the top of the food chain. I have won at every single level that I've ever played. He has four rings. I have 12. When he was nine, I was the only mom in the gym with all these men who were saying, 'Oh, you need to have him in this or that.' And I'd say, 'Excuse me? I got this. You're a weekend warrior. I did this thing! Google me!' Being a single mom, training my son to be a basketball player, I felt that I trained him for life because that's what sports is. It's a reflection of life. I could be down by 30 points in the third quarter and go for 40 and win the championship. Our motto is: you never want to get in a championship game and say, 'I coulda-shoulda-woulda…I should have run a little more, I could have lifted more weights.' You should be able to say, 'I put in all the work, Ma.' And then, if your best is not good enough, I'm not mad at you. But never say you didn't put in the work.

"I had a praying mother. She was a visionary. She always prayed and spoke things into existence: 'You are going to college. You will be successful.' And she always set standards: 'This is my house. Nobody comes in my house with a C. This is the standard. If you are a custodian, you better be the best custodian there is. Whatever you are, you are the top of the food chain. You're tall, hold your shoulders back, you're beautiful. You are my children.' That was the power of my mother's voice. As a mom you speak life into your children. I tell people, 'There's the Constitution of the United States, and there's the Constitution of Diane McGee.'

"I probably made some mistakes, but I tell my kids, 'I put you at the door. I gave you every ounce of me to put you at the door, but you're the one that had to kick it open.' That's all I can do, and I did it the best I knew how. When I knew better, I did better. That's my motto as a mother: when I knew better, I did better.

"My son tells me that I don't cry a lot. I said, 'Son, I do cry. But if there is spilled milk on the floor, crying is not going to get the milk up. You've got to get a mop.' When we navigate the world, we've got to fight for our children. I've got to advocate and I've got to fight for mine. I don't really care what other people do. I wasn't sure I was always doing it right. But as mothers, that comes with the territory. No matter if you have money or a big house or if you don't, you're always wondering, *Am I doing the right thing?* I just think that comes with motherhood. *Is it enough? Am I feeding him right?* JaVale had ADHD, and I was always up at the school, and because I'm an African American single mom, I would hear them starting to use that as an excuse and I'd say, 'No, don't give him a crutch! He has a responsibility to do what he's told, to be the best, and you do not need to give him an excuse. Life does not work like that.'

"All of us come to the table with something, but I don't allow him to allow anything to stop him from his destiny. Even from the standpoint of…people control their pronouns, well, I've always controlled his adjectives. I would go into the school, and people would say, 'He's arrogant.' I'd say, 'I'm sorry, this is *my* son. Do you think you could use *assertive*? Or *go-getter*? Not *arrogant*.' They'd say, 'Well, other mothers don't think like you.' Well, what does that have to do with me? For that child right there, he's my son, and this is what he needs. And I would advocate. And at the end of the day, I tell all mothers: 'No one is going to advocate for yours that came from your womb and your umbilical cord like you.' I call it the 'Umbilical Cord Anointing.' No matter how hard the world gets, no matter how much money you make, no matter how many people like you or don't like you, who loves you? Your mother will always love you. I've always told my kids that. When nobody else has your back, who's got your back? Your mother. And always understand that there is a universal law: always love and take care of your mom.

"Recently, I was diagnosed with stage four breast cancer. My son came with me to the diagnosis. And I said, 'Son, I appreciate you taking off work and taking time to go to this doctor's appointment to hear this.' And he said, 'Ma! What are you thanking me for? This is what I'm supposed to do. I'm your son. You're my mother. Everything that I am is because of you. Don't ever thank me for that ever again in life.' True story. And praise the Lord, two years later, I was cancer free. But when he said that, it brought tears to my eyes. And my daughter Imani would go to all my doctor's appointments with me, and she had a binder with her, and every time I'd ask a question, she would write down whatever they'd say. Both of my kids, they just came through, like, 'We got this.'

"I tell everybody: the best things I have ever done in my life is giving birth to JaVale McGee and Imani McGee-Stafford. When people asked me what I wanted to be when I grew up, I just said I wanted to be a mom. I do celebrate that mommy thing. I also celebrate my children because I'm extremely proud that they took their own journeys. I was just the root, but they built the tree that changed the world. My children are change agents. And that's really all we want as mothers: that they find their own destiny, that they set their goals and master them, and that they are good ambassadors to the world. That's what every mother wants.

"I'm a grandmother now, and they call me *Glamma*. The other grandmamas may do things one way. I'm like, okay, I'm a single

60-year-old that looks 40. I have the kids, I don't have the kids, I don't have to be there all the time. I'm not that type of grandmother. That ain't me. I've never put myself in a box. I do all the stuff I need to do. There's Glamma stuff. I go to all the birthdays, I spend weekends, I set up Glamma Time on my calendar. Then other times maybe I can't make it. And if I hear, 'I can't believe you can't do this. You're the grandmama!' I'm like, 'Okay, you'll get over it.' When I was a mother, I would drop everything. The only thing I would do for myself was to have bubble baths after the kids went to bed. And I'd put a sign on the door that said, 'Do not interrupt me unless there is a fire or somebody died.' And then I'll wait to call the coroner! You have to have time for yourself to regenerate. And I would have my gospel music and a bubble bath with candles.

"You have to put some time in for yourself before you give out, or we become emotionally, spiritually, and physically depleted. And mothers have to be okay with: this is my time. A lot of mothers don't fight for that. I have a lot more bubble baths now. And I travel more. In this season of my life, the cup is for me. I'm going to bless everybody from the overflow. But the cup is for me. I've paid my dues and raised my children. I'm blessing everybody from the overflow from the saucer."

6
DEBBIE ANTONELLI

The soundtrack of women's basketball has been elevated with Debbie Antonelli's analysis for nearly four decades. She played basketball at North Carolina State, developing a special relationship with her Hall of Fame coach, Kay Yow, that would ultimately influence many things in her life, including Antonelli's approach to motherhood. Yow endured a long battle with breast cancer that eventually took her life in 2009, but her legacy lives on through the Kay Yow Cancer Fund—for which Antonelli is a lifetime board member.

Antonelli became the first female analyst to call an NCAA men's tournament game in more than 20 years, and her work has been recognized at the highest level. In 2022 Antonelli was inducted into the Women's Basketball Hall of Fame and two years later she entered the Naismith Hall of Fame as one of the Curt Gowdy Media Award winners. Antonelli and her husband, Frank, have three boys—Joey, Frankie, and Patrick—and Antonelli is definitely in her element as a boy mom. There is one Tom Petty song, in particular, that, thanks to Antonelli, you will never hear the same way. So, there is laughter, but there's also so much authenticity and truth, especially when it comes to her family and her experiences with her middle son, Frankie, who was born with Down syndrome.

"When Frankie was born, we didn't immediately know that he had Down syndrome. The doctor took three visits to my room to tell us. We had no knowledge, not any indication at all that something wasn't right. Everything in the pregnancy was great. There were no problems with my son Joey, who was two-and-a-half years older. So once we found out, I struggled a lot. I went through the motions. I'm not proud of it, but it was such a shock to me. It took awhile to believe that God had chosen us. That's the way that I look at it now, but it took me a while to get there. My mother always told me that I didn't do something wrong; I did something right, which was very encouraging, but I needed something more.

"Frankie was about nine months old when I went to the 1998 NCAA women's Final Four. My former coach, Kay Yow, had led North Carolina State there for the first time in program history. I had a 30-year relationship with my coach from being a junior high camper, to being recruited and playing for her, and then, of course, covering her through my professional career. She had a huge influence on me. We got to talking, and she said, 'How are you doing?' And I said, 'I'm fine, I'm all right.' She said, 'No, how *are* you?' And after a minute I finally said, 'I'm not doing so well, actually. I'm having a hard time.' She said, 'I bet finding out you have a child with special needs is a lot like finding out you have cancer. It's not something you plan for. You didn't know it was coming. You don't know why. I bet there are some similarities there. I bet at first you nursed the hurt. That's what happens when you have cancer. Everybody feels sorry for you. Then you curse the hurt, you're mad. *Why me? Why did our family end up with someone with cancer or why did we get a child with special needs?* Then you go and rehearse, you practice how to accept people's empathy. You don't want it, but it comes, and you don't like it, but it still comes. So you've got those three things—nurse, curse, rehearse, and then you reverse. You make a choice. Like drawing a line in the sand and saying, 'You know what? I'm not going to let cancer beat me. I'm going to come up with a game plan and put my very best effort forward to beat this opponent. I'm going to treat it just like any other game plan that I do as a basketball coach.'

"When I heard her say that, it instantly clicked. She said, 'reverse,' and it was like the light went on for me. I went home to Frank and I said, 'That's it. No more wallowing around. No more crying. No more mad. No more can't figure it out, don't know why. Now I'm moving forward and I am going to give Frankie every opportunity and I don't care who's in my way.' It definitely had a little bully mentality to it.

"But I think that came from all my years of being a competitive athlete playing at the highest level and not taking no for an answer in my own training or fitness. I'm doing it right now training for my fundraiser.

This is so Debbie! She'll be talking about one thing and then—boom—she'll tie it into something else, like her fundraiser. Debbie is a national spokesperson and parent advocate for special education, and each year she hosts her "24 Hours Nothing But Net" fundraiser for the Special Olympics. She makes 100 free throws every hour for 24 hours straight and in 2024 she surpassed over one million dollars raised for Special Olympics. (You can go to 24HoursNBN. com to donate.) It's an honor for me any time that I get to team up with Debbie, be it supporting her fundraiser or calling a game together, and finding good teammates was definitely part of Debbie's game plan when it came to her family.

—J.H.

"The competitiveness, the athletic model, the coaching model, it all resonated with me. When I heard that from Coach Yow, that's when I thought, *You know what? That I can do. I can put a game plan together and can make sure I get the right people on the team.* It was an amazing turnaround. I'm forever grateful for her.

"You have to have a really good partner, and your partner has to understand your drive, your passion, the intangibles, plus the demands that the job has and the travel that's involved. Sure, we miss out on some things, but I've never felt an overarching sense of guilt. I have three boys, my husband's a great man, and I know that my boys are going to be great men because they spent a little extra time with him. And they saw what would be considered non-traditional things taking place. I always told Frank that there's not many things that come with being a parent that I do that he can't do except for some of the early stuff. But changing diapers, keeping a schedule, making lunch, getting the kids to school, coming home, making dinner, anyone can do that. And everyone should be doing it.

"Now, I will say, I never let anybody say 'Mr. Mom' in front of me because I don't think that's a thing. Frank was never 'Mr. Mom.' I'm the mom; he was being the dad. So we shared those responsibilities. We've always found a rhythm, not a balance. If the definition of balance is being 50/50, then we as moms know that ain't happening because I don't think I've ever had a day off! I make all the decisions. It feels like that anyway. It feels like I'm responsible for everything inside the house and outside the house. My motto is: build, serve, empower. I use those three words to guide all of my decisions. I feel like I am the CEO of my own little company. It's my basketball schedule, plus my camps—I do three weeks of girls-only sports camps—plus the fundraiser, plus all the boards, plus the kids. They're young men now, but still I max out my day. It's fulfilling because I'm doing a lot of things to help other people, but they also empower me to keep going.

"I have a full schedule, but I don't complain about my schedule because I choose it. There have been times when I'd be gone for three weeks straight, and I'd keep extra clothes at my parents' house so I could swing through there and change. Basketball season is busy, but that's by design. I worked the first 28 years of my career without a guaranteed number of games in my TV contract. So if there was a chance to work, I wanted to work. That's part of the reason that I only did basketball because if I had tried to do other sports, I would never have been home. I'd roll hard for five or six months—the season is longer now—and then I'd be home.

"In the earlier days, when the boys were like 12, 10, and five, there was a lot going on. They were all in school—three different schools, three different schedules—and I was always on the early flight home. If there was a 5:00 AM flight, I was on it. And with Frankie I would usually head straight to the school. I made sure that I had a visible presence there. I wanted to see that they were providing the right resources, that they were doing the IEP [individualized education program] the right way, that they were having the right attitude and the willingness to help him succeed. Any decisions regarding Frankie academically through the IEP process were all based on my schedule. There were no decisions that were made that I did not have full control over. I would bring Frank in only when I needed a hairy eyeball. I would tell him, 'Just stare at them. I'll talk; you stare.' And he did a good job of it! He would kick me under the table sometimes when he thought I went too far, and I'm sure I did, but it was worth it.

"I put a system together of communication where if Frankie was going from third grade to fourth grade and he was going to be working with new people, I would bring the people from last year and the people from this year together and I'd take them all out to dinner. I'd say, 'Okay, let's manage this right here outside the official IEP process so you guys can tell them what you need and how we're going to do this.' I did it like a head coach. I was the coach, and they were on the team, and if they didn't do their job, then I cut them from the team. There were a lot of tough times in IEP meetings—some went my way, some did not—but I never let them off the hook. They knew that I wasn't messing around. When Frankie got into seventh grade, I realized that there were programs that would allow him to go to college. So I created a different IEP, flow chart, and everything that was focused on what he would need to get into those programs. [Authors' note: Frankie wound up attending Clemson University through ClemsonLIFE, a program tailored to individuals with intellectual disabilities. Debbie also pushed her alma mater, North Carolina State, to create a similar program.]

"I think being very aggressive in a very kind way would be my advice to any parents of a child with special needs because there was no sacrificing Frankie. Either you figure it out as a teacher, find someone who can help you figure it out, or you're not going to be around very long. I also took care of people around the school. The maintenance guys and the lunchroom ladies, they all got T-shirts and stuff at Christmastime. I would give then that signal, pointing two fingers at my eyes, pointing them at theirs. They knew to keep an eye on my guy. I had eyes on the ground at all times.

"I was on it with everything with Frankie and I'm glad that I was. And now all of those people can celebrate along with us the incredible success he's having living independently with support. It's what you want. It's what we all strive for. He has a really fun life with a lot of friends and he has two jobs and he's doing really well. That's what I hope every mom of a child with special needs will have—incredible hope and opportunity if they plan for it and they have a vision for it and they're realistic about it. I was realistic. When my friends would say, 'My daughter who has Down syndrome is being included in the biology class, and they're modifying the curriculum, and she learned how to memorize the periodic table.' I'd be like, 'Oh, that's wonderful.' But then I'd think to myself, *Who the hell cares? Frankie's never going to work in a lab or have a job like that.* We don't need the periodic table. We're never going to use that. We need functionality—functional math, functional reading, functional responsibility, things that you can do realistically. That's what we worked on for the IEP, and that's what his life is.

"My other two boys and their friends are all better guys for learning how to adapt and tolerate and include—all the things that come with having a family member with special needs. And now that they're older, I'll say to them, 'My money is your money.' And both Joey and Patrick, they'll say, 'Mom, we know that this money is Frankie's money.' Because if something happens to me or Frank, one or both of them will make sure that Frankie's taken care of. That, to me as their mom, is very comforting.

"I think the boys overall see what an incredible life that Frankie has, but they also see those that don't have the same opportunities that he did. As a mom you're constantly building, teaching your kids to work hard and be a good teammate. Frankie has really been the centerpiece of everything in our family, and the other two are both builders and servants because of it. They understand that Frankie required a little bit more and they get it. It makes me really proud of them, that's for sure.

"My mother used to say to me, 'You're not going to remember the pain of labor and childbirth, but you'll remember all the great stuff.' That's true for everything in life. The hard work and the sweat equity, it's all part of the journey. You don't always remember the hard parts, but you remember the good stuff. [Authors' note: Oh, what a perfect ending this probably should be, but then there's that Tom Petty song we promised and part of the inspiration for the naming of Debbie's boat.]

"If we were out somewhere and we came home, I'd say, 'Guys, throw your clothes on the washing machine and free ball it to the showers.' And they would. Boys when they're little, that's what they do. They like to run around naked. As they grew up, I told them Tom Petty wrote a song just for them called 'Free Ballin.' I even had it painted on our boat. And we sing it at the top of our lungs. I mean the boys sing 'Fallin' and I sing 'Ballin.' But we have a good time with it."

7
ALYSIA MONTAÑO

AP Images

The girl with the flower in her hair. The pregnant runner. The mother who stood up for maternal rights. Author, advocate, ally. Alysia Montaño is all of these things and more. She is that teammate you want by your side because she is not afraid to stand out, speak up, and back up what she says with her actions. The statements Montaño makes are deliberate, powerful, and transformative, not only for her, but also for anyone facing similar barriers—women of color, female athletes, mothers. Picture her wearing a black T-shirt with white letters that says: "leader, risk taker, groundbreaker, instigator, &mother." The shirt is a nod to her non-profit, &mother, which she is in the process of rebranding to better reflect the next phase of its work. It's no coincidence that these powerful words embody both the company's mission and the attributes of the woman who created it.

Montaño wrote an op-ed in The New York Times *in 2019 that went viral and helped push companies like Nike to change their policies toward pregnant athletes. She ran at the 2014 U.S. Track and Field Championships eight months pregnant—not to win but to prove a point. She is a seven-time USA track and field national champion, and Montaño won two of those titles less than a year postpartum. She is at long last an Olympic medalist. In 2024, after a 12-year wait and the disqualification of two Russian runners for doping, she was awarded an Olympic bronze medal from the 2012 London Games. Montaño is a wife and proud mother of three— Aster, Lennox, and Linnéa. At the heart of everything that Montaño does is a strong sense of self-belief, one that grew brighter and stronger when she became a mother.*

"You live your life and discover things about yourself—your strengths, things you see in the world, things you cannot tolerate, things that maybe you have tolerated in the past and realize - never again. For me one layer of discovery was my womanhood. Walking into that and asking, 'Why is the world set up like this? What is happening here?' I see myself as a strong individual, a smart individual, a good friend, a kind person; I am a woman. And I see that there are these barriers that have nothing to do with my skillset, my talent, my intellect, my ability to be a kind person.

"I am also an athlete. I'm a born athlete. Part of me playing sports was because my mom was like, 'All right, here she is climbing the wall, and now the couch is a trampoline. Did she just do a backflip off of that? We've got to figure out what we're doing here.' I would always play with my brothers and cousins in our neighborhood, and they were actually super empowering. They were like, 'Alysia, she's first pick on our flag football team. We know we can depend on her in the final play. We're tossing her the ball in the final minutes when we play basketball. We know she's going to go and make that layup.' It was all this empowerment. But when we'd go up against other neighborhoods, those kids would be like, 'You're going to let her play? She's a girl!' That was an initial spark.

"As a runner I was known as the girl with the flower in her hair. That all started with the neighboring kids saying I couldn't play with them because I was a girl. So tackle this kid, put a flower in my hair. Say that I can't! I didn't believe that strength and femininity had to be two separate things, even though that's what society was telling me. Then being a Black woman and seeing those barriers that you walk up against where people are telling you that you cannot exist as you are. As a professional athlete, I was a seven-time national champion, and it was like they kept trying to pick another winner, pick someone else to focus on, someone who was a lighter version of me.

And I was like, 'Sorry, you just have to accept the Blackness!' I am as Black as can be and I'm out here, and we have to recognize this in how our sport supports—or does not support—darker-skinned people.

"Dare me not to dream about being at the forefront of change. That's the mentality that I've taken into motherhood. There were all of these stepping stones of growth that had nothing to do with what I brought to the table. It was more about how I showed up in the world. Once I became a mom, that was the final straw. It was like, 'Absolutely not. We are not about to do this for the entirety of my being, tell me who I can and cannot be because of how I present.' I know now to look for words like *pregnancy, postpartum*, and *maternity leave* in my contracts, but you don't think about that when you're a 20-year-old signing a new contract or starting a new job. The men in leadership told me, 'When you get pregnant, we're just going to pause your contract and stop paying you because you won't have the ability to be an athlete or a champion.' And I was like, 'Say that again? I dare you to tell me that I am no longer a valuable, strong human being because I am going to be a mother.'

"After that I went and I won nationals at six and 10 months postpartum. I broke an American record. I won a gold medal. I had proved everything. Yet when I told my corporate partners that I wanted to expand my family again and still make the next Olympic team, you could hear a pin drop. I was like, *What more do we need to do to prove ourselves?*

She is so committed to doing what's right. Doubt her, and that will only fan the flame. (Sorry, I had to work in an Olympic reference for her!) Although we certainly don't expect all our mothers to take on causes in addition to everything else, we appreciate everything this Tough Mother is doing to help women, moms, and working mothers. It's almost like she sees no other way.

—*A.L.*

"The invisible burden of motherhood is this load that mothers take on, where you are thinking through not only what you are doing for yourself and your child in the present moment, but also for the future. Then it has you thinking through the past, what wasn't, and what needs to be. It's just a lot to carry, especially when you recognize that we are carrying a lineage of women that have been walking up against walls that have been nearly impossible to break through. And when we talk about the burden of motherhood, this is what we inherit. Recognizing we are leaders, we can be instigators, we are risk takers, we are ground breakers. We are all of these things. I think that's also part of motherhood. Nothing is perfect. The perfection is the imperfection. And one thing that I say all the time is that we don't need problems we don't need. We don't need to not pay women for their work because they are pregnant or postpartum. We don't need to not have access to affordable childcare. We don't need to have women dying in childbirth.

"There are so many problems that don't need to exist. The one that walked up to me when I first became pregnant was 'What are you going to do after pregnancy?' This wasn't a problem to me; this is part of life. I'm going to be pregnant, have my baby, and continue my career. But not everyone thought that way. I competed at Nationals eight months pregnant because I wanted the people who created my contract to see what it looked like to be a woman in my condition showing up to work. I wanted to show them what this contract was telling me I had to do. So how would this contract need to look different? I wanted to make the invisible visible.

Then that helped me continue to advocate for change. We want to see maternity protection. So athletes don't have to show up the day before labor to a race they have written into their contract. And they need to be protected in their postpartum period to have their pay protected, their bodies protected, and their families protected.

"I see my kids in every part of the work that I'm doing. It's not just about your kids thriving. It's also about having them see me be strong and continue toward my goals and my dreams, seeing me be holistic, and seeing me help support and affect change for future generations. My daughter Linnéa was nine when I brought her with me to the Women's Sports Foundation's Annual Salute. She was like, 'I really see what you do, Mom. You are really helping girls and women in sport. You're helping them be better than it was.'

"After all, we are our kids' teachers and we are society's teachers, so to hear her say that, honestly, it took my breath away. I felt in that moment the relief of it all, like *This is not in vain.* It's a lot of work. It's a heavy load, and we do need to carry it together, but I felt her words in my heart. I felt a real swell of kinetic energy that continued to help push me forward. I can see that it matters to her, that I keep doing the work that I'm doing, that I am me. I am her mom, but I'm also me—the creative, the author, the writer, the nurturer, her mother.

"I also have two boys, and as much as we talk about how important it is for young girls, it's just as important for our young boys to see and elevate women in their empowerment. We are making it visible to them. We want them to be helpers, recognizing obstacles and helping us break them down. I didn't wait for anybody to tell me how strong I was. I feel like everyone who's ever known me knows that you can't put out my fire and I am also going to be somebody who won't put out yours."

PART III
SACRIFICE

—AIMEE

Sacrifice simply comes with the territory of motherhood, right? But having it all, as you'll hear from some of our Tough Mothers, is really more about defining "all" and focusing on what's most important for you and your family at the time. In the stories in this section, you'll read about vulnerability, pain, and even regret. Cheyna Matthews had to embrace the challenges of raising three children while both parents pursued careers as professional athletes. Women's Sports Foundation CEO Danette Leighton is incredibly grateful for her daughter, Olivia, but she also opens up about her biggest disappointment. *Good Morning Football* host Jamie Erdahl prioritized finding a job where she wouldn't have to get on a plane every week—even if that means the mom of three now welcomes her 3:00 AM wake-up calls. But everyone's sacrifice is their own. Big or small, yours is yours. Sometimes the choice is an easy one. And sometimes, well, not so much.

Unlike most of the working moms you're hearing from in this book, I would never call myself an athlete...well, actually, there's not a person I know who would call me that! But I've been a Tough Mother since 1992, the year of the Barcelona Summer Olympics. When I watched the Olympics Games on television between feeding and changing my newborn, I was in awe of the unique stories of each athlete, their remarkable qualities, and all the sacrifices they—and their families—made in order to compete at the Olympic level.

Fast forward four years, and I found myself working my first Olympics in Atlanta with my husband and four-year-old at home and me—pregnant with our second child—spending long days and way too many hours at the broadcast center. It hit me then that many of us behind the scenes were also making sacrifices in order to be there. And so were our families. I realized that we brought many of the same qualities to our work that the athletes brought to theirs (minus the athleticism, of course)!

I have had the incredible good fortune to work on the production of many big sporting events, including seven Olympic Games. It may sound glamorous, but I want you to know that those projects led to some of the biggest sacrifices I've ever had to make as a working mom. I was away sometimes for five weeks at a stretch and, no matter the time of year, I missed a lot. But I had a few tricks to make it easier on the kids. Sometimes, I would get a bunch of little gifts before I left, wrap them all up, and then have the babysitter pull out a present from Mom, especially when they were having a tough day. It helped to keep me a part of their everyday lives. You'll learn similar tricks from some of our Tough Mothers. Like Olympic swimmer Dara Torres, who used the same one I did, and Jenn took it a step further and set up some elaborate scavenger hunts for her girls.

Trust me: it hurt to be away from my family for so long, but I tried really hard to not let them see any of my sadness. I made it a point never to apologize for my job. I felt really fortunate—and still do—to be in a career that I absolutely love, and I wanted my children, Jay and Claire, to know that. Through the years they often came to my office to see where I worked, and they even went to a few Olympics with me. They saw that I was a part of a team, and even more importantly, they saw people appreciating what I did. I wanted them to know that when I wasn't with them, I was somewhere meaningful.

Back when I had my first kid in the early '90s, there weren't many working moms in my line of sight. I saw professional women who didn't have children, and there were my friends who decided not to go back to work after having their babies. While I respected everyone's choices, I missed having that sisterhood to turn to for guidance as I hit some of those inevitable challenges of being a working mom. I never doubted my path. But I often felt very alone. I knew going into it that it wouldn't be easy. I knew there would be plenty of sacrifices...by me, my husband, and, of course, our children. I just didn't realize it could be so difficult at times.

As a busy working mom, did I miss things while my kids were growing up? Absolutely. Those big holiday concerts in elementary school? I don't think I ever made it to one. But you know what I never missed? The Mother's Day plays in the classroom. I was not going to be the one mom that wasn't there for those. Wayne and I evaluated every one of those decisions and tried to find a way to minimize the impact on the kids. Like for the holiday concerts, he or the babysitter would go and try to record the parts our kids were in. We'd watch them together later and let the kids tell us all about it. I realized that I wasn't going to be a perfect mom or make the right choice every time and I had to accept that. I knew—and my family knew—that I was trying my best and that there was a thought process behind most of my decisions.

And even though my kids are mostly adulting these days, I still need a little reassurance once in a while that I did okay. So I'll sometimes look through the cards and notes they made me over the years. One of my favorites is one I found recently on the back of a notepad from when Claire was 10. It reads:

Aimee
If you ever find this, I want to let you know that you are the best
MOTHER EVER.
Xoxo
Claire...and probably Jay

Now that makes me smile.

Unfortunately, there is no recipe for success and no magic trick to soothe us from all the sacrifices we will ultimately make as working moms. There are just lessons and stories we share to reassure you, advise you, and prepare you. But most of all, to remind you that you can do this.

8
CHEYNA MATTHEWS

Cheyna Matthews played in two FIFA Women's World Cups with Jamaica (including the Reggae Girlz' historic first-ever World Cup appearance in 2019), won an NCAA championship at Florida State, played eight years of professional soccer in the NWSL, and created a line of athletic maternity apparel called Seeded Sweat. Cheyna and her husband, NFL receiver/tight end Jordan Matthews, have three sons—Josiah, Lionel, and Cairo. So they know all about the struggle of juggling parenthood and not one, but two professional sports careers. With uncertainty surrounding schedules, contracts, and even their living situations, there was plenty of sacrifice as both parents tried to follow their dreams while also supporting each other and their growing family. In fact, Cheyna and Jordan often use the phrase "ready, set, go!" to help motivate their kids to do chores or pick up toys. But those words could apply to mom and dad as well, especially Cheyna, for those times when she had to leave her family behind for work.

Cheyna didn't make her debut with Jamaica until after the birth of her first son and she continued to play both professionally and internationally after all three pregnancies. She made the decision to retire from soccer in 2023 but only after she pushed herself—often on her own miles away from her family—to represent Jamaica at the World Cup one final time.

I was in a contract year when I got pregnant with my third son—I think I was always in a contract year with my babies—and I thought I would just re-sign with my current team, Racing Louisville, when I came back. I had my son, Cairo, in July of 2022, but the club decided to go in a different direction. Our Jamaican national team coach was adamant that we all play professional soccer leading up to the 2023 World Cup, and I wasn't sure what I was going to do. I didn't have a team.

"In December of that year, we moved into our new home in Nashville, Tennessee, to be closer to family. Not long after that, I got an offer to join the Chicago Red Stars. I wanted to show how committed I was to getting back to soccer, especially coming back from having my third child, but I knew I couldn't uproot my family. We had their schools and childcare all set up in Nashville, and I wanted to make it as seamless as possible for them. So essentially, I just removed myself from the situation. I moved to Chicago and I had to leave the boys with their dad and grandparents in Nashville. They supported me. They were like, 'Hey, this is a World Cup year. We need to buckle down and do this.' But it was really tough.

"I had just worked my way into the starting lineup with Chicago when I got a freak ankle injury. I was out for almost six weeks. That was really lonely. When you're there to train and help your team, then you can't because you're facing an injury, and you're away from your family, it's hard. I would see them on weekends—they would come see my games or I would go home to them—but really between playing in the NWSL and the World Cup, I spent about six or seven months away from my family that year. It was challenging. I also knew that I would never do something like that again! It was a little easier to wrap my brain around what I was doing, just knowing that would probably be my last year playing professional soccer. My oldest son was going into kindergarten, and I wanted to be in one place for him.

"I am proud, though, that I didn't let becoming a mom stop me from accomplishing what I really wanted to accomplish. For so long it seemed like it had to be one or the other—keep playing or become a mom—or wait to have children until you're done with your career. But having three children in my eight-year career, I think I'm most proud that I was able to do it.

"We don't have enough moms that feel comfortable being in their field and having children. It is easier to have them after, but it's also totally doable to do it while you continue to play or go to work. It's an honor to raise these babies and also have a career doing what you love to do. And it does mean a lot to me to be an example; I think that's something that I realized later in my career. At first I was just trying to survive as a mother and as an athlete. And initially I felt like I had to keep those two parts of my life completely separate because I didn't want that to affect how I was viewed as a player. I wanted to just be viewed like everyone else. I didn't want to be the mom on the team. It was like he's my son, and this is my work. And with my first son, Josiah, I was playing in Washington, D.C., and I was able to do that. It was as seamless as it could have been. My husband, Jordan, was training there for his team during the offseason, we had a great nanny, and I hardly ever had to bring Josiah to any practices or anything.

"Now when I got to Louisville, it was a lot different. Jordan left for California for his job, it was just me and our two sons, and some days the babysitter I had would call or text me at 3:00 AM and say, 'Hey, I'm not going to make it tomorrow.' It was just very inconsistent. So when I had to start bringing my kids around more is when I started to realize the impact that it had.

[Authors' note: Before Mother's Day in 2021, Cheyna was back with her Racing Louisville team for the first time since having her second son, Lionel. Racing director of player experience and operations Brynn Sebring tweeted this: "THIS BADASS BREAST FED AT HALF TIME I AM IN AWE..."] "When I saw that tweet from Brynn, about me being a badass, I had to laugh. I remembered her saying almost those exact words to me as she saw it happening. But I didn't think what I was doing was anything that extraordinary. It was like, 'Yes, I'm a professional soccer player. And, yes, I'm a mom. I am using my body to help take care of my kids and be nourishing to them, but it's not a superpower; it's just motherly instinct.' Now, I never intended to breastfeed my son in a locker room at halftime. My mom was on the trip with me, and she was watching Lionel. But since I got hurt and wasn't playing, I figured I would just have her bring him to me and let me nurse him. I went into the hallway outside the locker room, pulled up one of the folding chairs, and fed him right there. That's when Brynn walked by and saw me, and it was good for my teammates to see, too. It gave them a fresh perspective on what motherhood really looks like. The rookies, especially, were like, 'I cannot believe you're doing that! I'm tired and I don't have a kid to take care of. You're doing it with a kid, traveling with him, you've got all this stuff to take care of.' It was kind of mind-blowing to them.

"I think with them seeing that, it not only grew the respect that they had for me, but also the respect that I had for myself, just being able to balance it all. More and more, I think we are starting to see athletes who are mothers coming back stronger than ever. I actually got the idea to start my own athletic maternity clothing line because I noticed there was a real need for it. It was a struggle for me when I was pregnant to find something that screamed: 'You are a badass! You can do this!' That was my goal with my brand, Seeded Sweat. For pregnant or postpartum women, I want to promote that edge and empowerment that you can have when you're working out. You need sports bras that actually support your breasts, leggings that come up over your belly and make you feel secure. The brand is all about empowering women and encouraging them that you can have babies and still play or work out.

It blows me away that through all of the different chapters of Cheyna's life so far, she's always stayed true to who she is. As an athlete. As a mom. As a pregnant woman. As a nursing mom. She's layered the roles on top of each other and, as she's gotten older, it seems she's realized the impact she can have on others. She shows us that you can be all these different things and that as a working mom, yes, you'll make sacrifices, but you never have to sacrifice who you are at your core. And yes, you can still be a badass!

—*A.L.*

"Motherhood doesn't change who you are. It doesn't change what you're capable of. That person—all that she is and all that she can do—is just as important to your kids as it is to you."

DANETTE LEIGHTON [9]

Danette Leighton is the CEO of the Women's Sports Foundation (WSF). So she knows all about empowering women. WSF was established in 1974 by tennis legend and women's rights activist Billie Jean King to advance the lives of women and girls through sports and physical activity. Leighton joined WSF in 2022 after close to a dozen years with the Pac-12 Conference, where she earned the title of chief marketing officer. She has worked in the NBA and WNBA, striving to succeed in a landscape often bereft of many other women executives. While she refers to herself as a "middle school dropout" because she quit playing softball in ninth grade, she's pretty sure she wouldn't have become a C-suite executive without sports. Leighton's now focused on making sure sports is seen as a "must have" not a "nice to have" for girls and women. As for herself and her family, Leighton has chosen to be very open about the sacrifices she's made for her career. And she wants other women to know that it doesn't have to be this way.

"**M**y daughter Olivia is the greatest gift I have ever had. She is my world, she is my everything, and I feel very lucky to have her. But I think I made choices about not expanding my family that were completely on me because I didn't know who to ask, what to ask, or how to be vulnerable. My biggest disappointment in life is that I only had one child. And that was completely my doing because I didn't know how to have another one and find the right balance with my work.

"Back then I was trying to prove something. I wanted to prove that I could be an executive in sports. I wanted to prove that I could do it and do it as well as my male counterparts. When I was an undergraduate at the University of Arizona, we had a high-ranking female executive within the athletics department. I saw her, and it was that if-you-see-her, you-can-be-her mentality, right? But I also realized that there weren't that many women, especially in higher positions. So I think part of my mentality was, *Oh my gosh, I have to be the best, perfect, most amazing role model for other women.* I didn't want anybody to ever see me fail. And I thought it was very hard to balance working in professional sports with having a kid. But I think in the end I sacrificed a lot and I put what I really wanted, which was to have a big family, last.

"Since then I have tried to be that person who is very transparent about the mistakes that I made, so that women who come behind me can have the courage to be vulnerable and go after what they really want. We shouldn't feel guilty about wanting to have a career and wanting to have a family, but we need a space and a community where you can have those conversations. I don't think I ever chose to be vulnerable enough to find that community. I had great women and moms around me—and great men as a matter of fact—but I was never open enough about how I was feeling. Then time passed, and it was too late. The advice that I tell people—and that I try to live by now—is that you have to live and work to your own personal values.

"If you know what that North Star is, and that North Star is that you want to have a big family, for example, you have to go have a big family and figure the rest of it out. But know that 'figuring the rest of it out' may not be exactly what you expected it to be. Be real about the fact that it's not simple. It may take a different way of mothering and it may take a village around you, and that's okay. I think you feel guilty when you have nannies and support and care. And I know not everyone has the ability to do that. But I think you have to be honest and transparent about the journey and don't feel guilty about whatever choice you make. Those that choose to stay home, that's an important decision. Those that choose to work, that's an important decision. Those that *have* to work, that's respect right there. But stop putting any negative connotation on any of those scenarios. All of them are fine, and all of them are going to require different types of support. But be less hard on yourself, open yourself up, and try to be more vulnerable.

"If you would have had this conversation with me when I was in my early 40s, when my daughter was like eight, I would have been very different. Much more like, 'Oh, I've got this!' But I'm also now a cancer survivor, which gives you perspective. [Authors' note: After a routine colonoscopy in 2023, Leighton was diagnosed with stage one colon cancer. Fortunately, because she discovered it early, she was able to treat it without chemotherapy and is now cancer free. Danette's PSA to all of us: don't hold off on scheduling your colonoscopy!] You want to talk about eye-opening. Once you get that diagnosis, the last thing you're worrying about is where you worked. The only thing you think about is your family, what's important to you, the people that are closest to you, and how you want to live the rest of your life.

"My daughter is bummed that she doesn't have siblings. That cuts deep because that was my choice and my biggest regret. But if I don't share it, then how is anybody else ever going to learn to do it differently? Maybe they don't try to be a big ridiculous planner like I was, to try to have everything perfectly in line, to try and have a child between a WNBA and NBA season. I mean, literally, that's what I did! I was a freak like that. I needed my life to be structured and planned out instead of just rolling with it. And sometimes you've just got to roll with it. I think that's still a work in progress for me. But I'm more in tune now to where my weaknesses are. I hold the mirror up a lot more than I used to.

"And my daughter has never been shy to tell me what she thinks. Olivia has always told it like it is, and I appreciate that about her. She is the exact independent woman that I wanted to raise. Sometimes, I'm like, *What did I do?* Ha ha, no, I've always had a very insightful daughter. When she was really little and I was working in Sacramento [with the Kings and Monarchs of the NBA and WNBA, respectively], she said to me, 'Mom you're never around. You're always working.' That was like a punch in the face, but I needed it. It took that for me to really evaluate what I was doing and to make some pivots in my career path. I loved my job in Sacramento, but I knew it was time for me to look for something different. I was able to continue to advance my career, but I took a conference job with the Pac-12 rather than a school or team job. I knew that I wouldn't have to be at a game every night, and that was a big reason why I made that pivot, so that I could be more present. I still traveled a lot, I wasn't that mom in the classroom bringing cupcakes, and I definitely had an army of moms around me to help, but I was more present.

"One of the things I've always had to work on, though, is switching into mom mode when I get home. My family will say, 'Stop being a manager. I'm your daughter. I'm your husband.' You have to know how to pivot back into the roles and recognize that your family is not your team. I love my job, I love what I do, and I do have a tendency to not know how to turn it off. So I think having somebody to check you—and I'm appreciative of my husband and my daughter for that—I think that's really important. You can have that career ambition, but you need to know how to turn it off and be a human again. Dial it down a notch. I think I didn't learn that very well until a lot later in life.

"Becoming a parent you're just constantly on this whole journey of *What the heck am I doing?* All of the angst I might have felt over not being that perfect mom, I think in the end my daughter would say that she loves that she was raised by a working mom. Those things that I used to think were hurting her or that made me a bad mom—like never being able to volunteer in the classroom or missing out on field trips—she'll look at me and say, 'What are you talking about? I just always saw you in a different light.' I think I put all that of that guilt on myself.

"A few years ago, Olivia said to me, 'Mom, you know we all call you Queen!' That was honestly the best comment I've ever gotten in my entire life. She kids around and calls me Queen, but she was doing it to say, 'I love that you are the way that you are.' And to hear that from your teenage daughter, you just kind of melt. So I think what I'm most thankful for is that all of the angst that I put into myself—it didn't screw her up. Or not yet, at least! I know I am a role model for her to go follow her passions and her dreams and to find that balance with work and family. I don't have any regrets in the end of how it all came to be; I just wish I would have added to the crew."

Wearing a sassy red jumpsuit a la pregnant Rihanna from Super Bowl LVII, Jamie Erdahl announced she was pregnant with her third child on live television. One of the co-hosts on NFL Network's Good Morning Football, *Erdahl said: "I am not going to be Rihanna, I am embodying Rihanna." Erdahl, who played basketball and softball at St. Olaf College in Minnesota, is a mother to three girls—Brooke, Avery, and Nora—all born in a span of less than six years. Before coming to NFL Network in 2022, Erdahl spent eight years at CBS Sports as a host and sideline reporter and worked her way up to becoming the network's lead reporter for its SEC football package. But as her family continued to grow, she became increasingly aware of which parts of her life she was willing to sacrifice for her job...and which ones she was not.*

"The holidays used to be the hardest for me. I love the holidays. I love being around my family, sharing time with them, celebrating. But I also work in sports. And sports, well, they don't really care about the holidays. In 2019 my first daughter, Brooke, was about four months old and I was assigned to cover the Iron Bowl [the annual Alabama-Auburn rivalry game] over Thanksgiving weekend. I think I left Thursday morning, the day of Thanksgiving. And you can do all you want in the days before—see your family, squeeze in a meal—but you still feel the absence of it on the actual day. My family and I have learned how to adjust—as all great teams do—but thinking back on this particular experience, I was struggling. You're on the road and you know your child is celebrating her first Thanksgiving without you. *That's* where you feel like you should be, but instead you're driving a rental car around Alabama to go eat chicken wings. I had such pangs of sadness being away from my baby.

"And here's where the real challenge is: in those moments of sadness, you cannot let yourself spin it forward too much and think, *Is this going to be my whole life?* It's too overwhelming. Motherhood is hard enough to endure one moment at a time, much less letting yourself get carried away thinking about all of the things that *could* happen in the future. But I will say that it planted a seed in my mind.

"I tried to draw inspiration from other women I saw making it work as mothers in sports. Laura Rutledge [another one of our Tough Mothers] and I had been keeping in touch. And I remember when she came back from having her baby, Laura was coming off her pregame show on SEC Network, I'm getting ready to start our CBS game broadcast, and we just hugged and were like, 'We're actually doing this! It's happening!'

"One thing that helped me was scheduling. I'm convinced that when you have a child, your three most dominant personality traits emerge. One of my three is scheduling. Every football game, there were essentially 10 men involved in me having a seamless pumping setup before a major network broadcast. So you know I had to plan that well. I also chose to just be very upfront about it. There was no dancing around the subject. Anyone I ran into—and in hindsight maybe I was a little *too* forward—I'd say, 'I just had a child and I'm breastfeeding.' I just wanted to put it out there in the universe and I wasn't about to let anyone stop me from doing it, including, apparently, members of the secret service.

"We found out that the president was going to be in attendance for one game that we were covering, and that meant I had to make some adjustments to my pumping plans. I had been warned that it would be difficult to get in and out of the stadium. So we found a place inside for me to pump. But let me tell you: those secret service agents, they wanted to inspect everything, including my pump. I was like, 'Don't touch this stuff! I will show it to you.' It's funny how you learn to advocate for yourself. I would never have been so assertive in the past! But in this moment, I was like, *I don't care who you work for. This thing is mine. It's for my baby. It's not anything dangerous, so I will assist you. You will not run your hands all over this machinery that is feeding my child.*

"Most of the time, I'm a go-with-the-flow type of person. I was amazed at how this journey of motherhood just gave me this boost. My mom is from Philadelphia, and she calls it, 'Having the Philly in her.' I think becoming a mother, feeling like my baby—or my baby's pump, in this instance—was being threatened, gave me some of that 'Philly.' It just came out of me. It felt like that edginess that I had playing sports emerged again. That competitiveness came out, like, *You, sir, will not beat me! You will not deter me or mess with my breast pump!*

"When football season ended that year, I was so amazed that I had gotten through it, pumping and breastfeeding all the way. I couldn't believe that I had done it, like, *I accomplished that!* And there were many times that I thought I might quit. I would take myself off the hook when I was home every Sunday and say, *Do I want to do this again next weekend?* I literally just took it one week at a time like that. It can seem like this uphill battle that is insurmountable if you think about trying to do it for six months, a year, or whatever your goal may be. I'd ask, *Can you breastfeed this child today? Great. Do that. Do they need half breast milk, half formula tonight because you need a little break? Okay. Just do that then.* The breastfeeding was so important for me, though, not only to feel a connection to my baby while I was on the road, but to also help me not experience as much profound guilt. I kind of felt like, *I'm doing my best for you here, kid. I'm giving you the best that I can give you even when I'm not around you.*

"I did make some changes as our family continued to grow. We had our first two kids within 22 months of each other, and when I was doing sideline, my husband and I never saw each other. He traveled for work. So he would often leave on Sunday night and come back on Thursday, and during football season, I would leave on Thursday and come back on Sunday morning. It was so hard on both of us. So when the opportunity came to move to a hosting role with NFL Network, I realized, *I won't have to get on a plane anymore.* And that was so appealing to me. I will wake up at any time as long as it means that I don't have to get on a plane. With our show moving to L.A., I'm getting up at 3:00 AM and I don't really care because I'd probably be getting up at 3:00 AM with a newborn anyway!

"The first six years of your kids' lives are so impactful and just seem to go by so fast. I decided that I was going to do everything in my power to be around for as much of that as I could. It's still hard but in a different way. At least now my husband and I are around each other more, and we can look each other in the eye and say, 'This is insane!' And it's not over FaceTime, where you're on the road somewhere, feeling so helpless while the other person is doing all the work at home.

"We've also gone through some scary moments as a family that have changed me, and that have affected my perspective on things. My oldest, Brooke, had viral meningitis when she was six weeks old and she got really sick. She was hospitalized, and that was like my first big parental shift. I had to sit there with her and hold her down while she cried as they put a needle in her back. Then with my youngest, Nora, I had to have an emergency C-section because the cord was prolapsed [dropping down early], and it was also wrapped around her neck. I shared this post on Instagram: 'To myself who thought everything was fine until it wasn't. To my husband who met my petrified tears with calm and strength despite his own terror. To my nurse and her ability to identify a problem that got our healthy baby girl out 6 minutes later. To my doctor who rode on the bed with me to the OR and her powerful voice that commanded a bad situation. To my anesthesiologist who advocated one last time on my behalf to not be fully sedated. To my mom who never once let her fear ripple out onto our little girls at home that there could be a problem brewing. To my sister who had a plane ticket booked before knowing the outcome of my emergency c-section. To sweet baby Nora James who cried one loud healthy cry right when she could to tell me she was ok. To my body...Thank you. We did it. That was hard. My family is complete. Time to rest. ♥ Despite the cord being prolapsed and around her neck - Nora was born healthy and beautiful on 3/30. We love you so much.'

"Everything feels less intense now. When it's a matter of your baby dying and all the things that could have happened—that didn't—I'm just like, *Man, coloring on the wall doesn't feel that bad anymore!* I think every working mom would say that she wishes there was one extra day in the week. Whether that's spent getting a little extra work done, a little extra parenting done, a little extra sleep done, I just wish there was more time because I really love everything that I signed up for. Between having the kids and having a job and being myself, I just wish I had more time.

Amen, sister! Speaking of which...at this point, Jamie hops up to grab her two-month-old, Nora. Seamlessly, without taking a breath or missing a beat, she starts breastfeeding her baby. Pretty fitting that while we are having this conversation about balancing it all and motherhood and wishing for more time in the day, she is just multitasking like the Tough Mother she is. Respect.

—J.H.

"It's important to remember, too, to stay true to who you are. When you have a child, especially as a new mom, it can feel like it takes over 100 percent of you. But I think whatever your job is—if it's motherhood or a career or both—you are allowed to save 10 percent of yourself for *you*. You were probably a pretty great person before you had a kid, and I bet you still are."

PART IV
RESILIENCE

—JENN

Athletes are often perfectionists. They push and drive and have this incredible will to succeed because failure in any form is not an option. But all athletes—and mothers—inevitably learn that it's not *if* you fail but when. What is motherhood if not a never-ending test of trial and error? And what athlete has ever had a journey free of any setbacks or letdowns? It's not the failures that define you as a mother or an athlete, but what you choose to do with them. How resilient can you be when shit gets hard?

Paralympic gold medalist Alana Jane Nichols likes to call it "embracing the suck." Heather Mitts Feeley, a three-time Olympic gold medalist in soccer, speaks about using a "Gold medal mindset" in both sports and life. I'd say the Phelps family knows a thing or two about gold medals, and while sisters Hilary and Whitney Phelps did not pursue swimming all the way to Olympic glory like their brother Michael, they have their own powerful journeys of resilience to share. And we can't forget about Hall of Fame broadcaster—and my mentor—Andrea Kremer. As she shares in her chapter, Andrea persevered through moments in motherhood that brought her to her knees—not to mention the fact that she went into labor 3,000 miles from home.

These dueling demands of work and family will make you question your worth, and we will all inevitably ask the question: *Am I good enough?* Especially when we encounter what we feel to be failure. We have to fight the perfectionist paranoia in our heads and move on. In my younger days, I never would have believed that. In my own big-fish, small-pond youth, I was a multi-sport athlete, a good student, and, yes, a perfectionist. I graduated as salutatorian from my high school. (If my GPA had been ⁶⁄₁₀ of a point higher, I would have been the valedictorian—not that I'm still hung up on that or anything.) But as I looked out at life beyond my small town, I learned that I would have a lot more opportunities to figure out how to handle failure.

More specifically, I had to *dare* to fail. My mom used to say those words to me, and looking back now, I realize how important that was. And how brave and resilient *she* was. My parents divorced when I was a senior in high school after nearly 25 years of marriage. My mom had to figure out how to restart her life in her mid-40s while raising two kids and trying not to let her hurt affect us. She had never been a runner, but she started going on these long runs, where she would use that time to grieve. When she came home, she was everything that we needed her to be and more.

I know now how difficult that time was for her. It hurts my heart to even think about it. But my mom persevered through that pain to become an even greater version of herself. It took time and a lot of tears and healing, but she did it. She moved to a new house, started building a new community, and is now happier than she has ever been. She is a respected artist in the Adirondacks, she leads hikes through the mountains pointing out wildflowers, and she is absolutely the best mother and grandmother in the world. I was able to dream big because my mother showed me the way, and she gave me permission to fail.

When I was a freshman working through soccer two-a-days in sweltering Atlanta heat, my mom reminded me: "Dare to Fail." As a rising sophomore wondering if my family could afford to send me back to Emory for another year, my mom wrote letters requesting financial aid and said to me again: "Dare to Fail." Those words drive me as an adult, too, as a woman daring to make her way into a man's world of sports broadcasting and as a mother trying to raise two children while spending so much time away from them on the road.

So often you only see or hear the success stories. I made the soccer team. I am a play-by-play announcer. I have two amazing daughters. But there have been plenty of failures, too: getting cut from the basketball team my freshman year in college, losing my job calling women's basketball games because I wasn't yet good enough, crying my fears out to my husband that I am not a good mom.

Failure as an end product is not an option for me in any facet of my life. But I discovered that failure as a part of the journey is a necessary tool to build resilience and fuel our drive. Sometimes we just need that reminder that it is okay to dream, that we can push ourselves beyond what we—or others—think we can do, that we Dare to Fail.

11

ALANA JANE NICHOLS

Alana Jane Nichols is a five-time Paralympian and three-time Paralympic gold medalist. She is the first American female to win gold in both the Summer and Winter Olympic Games, in wheelchair basketball and alpine ski racing, respectively. There is no question that Nichols is a gifted athlete, but her teenage dreams of athletic glory never included a wheelchair or the prefix Para before Olympian. Nichols would discover how resilient she really was after one singular, life-changing moment at the age of 17 involving a snowboard, a miscalculated jump, a backflip, a hidden rock, a scream, and a shattered spine. Nichols can still take your breath away when she tells the story of this moment, but on these pages, she opens up about life as a mother. She and her husband, Roy Tuscany, who is also a disabled athlete, have a son, Gunnar, who was born in 2019. Nichols' experiences as a disabled athlete may have built up her resilience, but she has relied on her ability to bounce back plenty more times as a mother.

"I tell my son that I was born the day that he was born, that I'm growing alongside him as a parent and as a mom. And what a test of patience that is! Everything that is presented in a single day is the curriculum of this life. I'm learning from every moment just like he is. The challenge is to stay open to those little learning moments, and for me that ties back a lot to being an athlete. As I was training for any one of my three sports, I never expected myself to be perfect. [Authors' note: Oh, by the way, Alana also picked up sprint kayaking.] I knew that the process involved making mistakes and so I try to remind myself of that as I'm parenting, like this is another sport. It's probably the most extreme sport that I've done, to be honest, and I was a ski racer! It is really so imperfectly perfect in a lot of ways.

"It's letting go of the expectations of how you think everything should go and just being really present with what is. I think every mom does this, but you get so hyper focused on things like getting out the door and being on time, and this little being you're rushing around doesn't have any idea about time. They don't know why or what's going on. All they feel is anxious because you're rushing. There are these constant reminders of what matters most, and the question becomes 'Are you paying attention?' Because the more you push against the natural flow of what's happening, the harder it's going to be. You kind of just need to let the day unfold sometimes.

"In that way it's a spiritual journey for me. It's a spiritual practice of being present. And there's no other more spiritual practice in my life experience than being an athlete. There are only so many things you can control leading up to a competition or a performance, and then you trust in the process of how you've prepared and what you've done. That's how you get into the flow state and that's how you stay in the present.

"I know now that every day I spent training for my Paralympic sports, I was also preparing myself to train for motherhood. I was developing this sense of openness to the outcome. I learned through trial and error that when you only focus on the end result and you don't win—and only one percent of the population wins a gold medal—you wind up asking yourself, *What was it all for?* You have to focus on the process.

"There are just all of these little bite-sized nuggets of experience from sports that I apply to my everyday motherhood journey. In that first year of motherhood when I was beyond exhausted and we went through sleep regressions and all of those things, I just told myself: *Remember when you were a ski racer and you told yourself you could do anything for one more minute?* And then I just sat there in the dark, breastfeeding for one more minute. That's how I got through those hard moments.

From the moment I started working in sports, I've been inspired by athletes' ability to push themselves. But this right here, this might be one of the most beautiful and relatable examples of that. So for any of you mamas wondering if you can get through this moment—whatever it may be for you—we hope these words from Alana will help you see that you absolutely can.

—A.L.

"I'm grateful for my experiences both before and after my injury because I know what it means to work hard and I also realized I have more gas in the tank than I thought. And that's part of the mental struggle that you go through as a mom, feeling out of gas, and you're like, *You've got this.* I learned that through all of those hard workouts, all of those tough moments in competitions where I had to push through, and it made me a lot stronger. We used to say 'embrace the suck,' like you know this workout is going to suck so bad, but you embrace it and you just deal with it. And that's my advice to parents, too! Sometimes in this busy life of ours, it's going to suck, but we're also going to be better for having gone through it. My husband and I both travel, and I know the tension and bittersweet feeling of having my own life—and enjoying that—while at the same time feeling a little guilty and just sad because I miss my kid. It's both/and, not either/or. I just dropped my son and husband off at the airport, so this house is empty. I'm like, *I love this* and *I miss that guy!* We as mothers need to embrace the 'both/and,' and that has definitely been a process for me.

"I really encourage new moms to give themselves grace. I remember when I first made the Paralympic basketball team and I was so raw. I was literally just pushing around the court like a chicken with my head cut off. I did not know what I was doing. And I remember one of my mentors at the time, and she'd say, 'Hey, you're the shit, Al. You're the shit! You've got this!' And I'd say, 'Okay. Okay! I believe you…kind of!' I needed to hear that in those moments, and new moms need to hear that, too. I eventually believed it, but you need to surround yourself with a community of people. You need to be on a team. You need to have those people in your life that see you're doing something that's really hard, so they can remind you of how bad ass you are. [Authors' note: Yes, that is exactly what we're doing right now, reminding all of you working moms reading this book: "You are the shit! You are a badass! You've got this!"]

"You can do hard things. You can do whatever it takes. You're a mother, you have everything you need to get through this and to do it really well, too. There are days when you're going to feel like you're not doing great, but those are also part of the process. And it's not a matter of if but when you will make a mistake. That's something that I learned from Dr. Becky Kennedy [author of *The New York Times* bestseller *Good Inside*] who is a great resource. But the thing is, you can repair your mistakes at any time. Even if you're a mom that has adult children that maybe didn't feel they were seen in a certain way and they bring that to your attention, you have an opportunity to repair and rewrite the story.

"There are days when I don't wake up and meditate and set myself up for success, and I'm not my best self. Then I snap at my son and have to say, 'Hey, bud, I'm sorry about that. I just didn't do my best. And that's okay, too.' He learns a lot from that, and I learn a lot, and the humility involved is so powerful. If you repair, it's like that's all that matters. It's not an excuse to make mistakes, but it just makes the humanity of it all rise to the surface rather than trying to be a perfect mom. We're kind of redefining what it looks like to be a great mom.

"As for becoming a mom with a disability, it's uncharted territory for each person. I can share my lived experience, but each disability is so nuanced and different. Parenting with a disability is like traveling to Europe in a wheelchair. It can feel so inaccessible. You don't know where there are going to be stairs and you can't plan for it, but just go! It will work out. There could be these really handsome men standing around at the bottom of the stairs just waiting to carry you up!

"If you overthink it your whole life, you'll never get there. There has to be an element of risk that you take going into it where you just have to trust yourself and know that whatever it takes you can provide for your child. There's this real beauty in embracing the interdependence that comes with being disabled. For able-bodied people, that comes later in life when you need somebody's help with something whether it's because you're aging or you have an injury or whatever. But when you're disabled, that beauty of blessing somebody else with the opportunity of assisting you is built in. Embrace it.

"I remember wondering how I was going to travel by myself with my baby. I need an aisle seat and I would usually just wear Gunnar in a baby carrier onto the plane. But one trip the transfer from my wheelchair to the seat felt a little sketchy. I didn't want to fall or land on him or whatever. So I ended up having to hand my baby to the flight attendant, and you would not believe the joy in her eyes from getting to hold this newborn! And I was like, *Okay, we've got this.* It's a dance of interdependence if you can let go of all the judgment around it. For me because I do have a disability, I didn't have much choice in the matter. So I didn't have any shame around it. Remember the classic line: 'It takes a village to raise a child.' You don't have to do it all alone. Sometimes even able-bodied moms may just need to hand their kids off to somebody and go take a nap."

12
ANDREA KREMER

Andrea Kremer may well be the first working mother in the history of the National Football League. If others existed before her, she didn't see them. Women were scarce when Kremer started covering the NFL, and working moms even more so, but Kremer blazed a trail of her own. She grew up as a little girl who loved football, even sleeping on sheets covered with NFL logos and helmets, and eventually worked her way into the Hall of Fame. Kremer is a member of the Pro Football Hall of Fame, the National Sports Media Association Hall of Fame, and the Sports Broadcasting Hall of Fame. She is the chief correspondent for NFL Network and was a correspondent for HBO's Real Sports with Bryant Gumbel. *Through her time as a reporter with ESPN and NBC, she has covered more than 25 Super Bowls. But she has a particularly memorable story about Super Bowl XXXIV and the lasting lessons it taught her about both work and motherhood.*

"I was eight months pregnant when I headed across the country from my home in Los Angeles to the Super Bowl in Atlanta. I was having dinner with my boss and his wife about a week before the game when I lean over to my boss' wife, Betsy, and I go, 'Oh my God, I hear women become incontinent at the end of pregnancy, but I'm peeing on myself!' We get in the car, same thing is happening. I get to my hotel and am standing at the elevator bank to go up to my room, and these people come up to me and ask for my autograph. So I'm signing autographs while I'm peeing on myself. Thank God I was wearing black pants! I get to my room and tell my husband John what's happening, and he says, 'Your water broke. Call the doctor.'

"So he gets on a flight—the last flight that landed before they closed the Atlanta airport due to an ice storm, by the way—I make it to the hospital, and then we wait. I start doing work, and one of the nurses says to John, 'Is your wife gonna make time to have this baby?' I was recording voice tracks for stories that would run leading up to the Super Bowl. And yes, I did in fact make time to give birth to my son, Will. In a hospital 3,000 miles from home. Four days before the Super Bowl.

"When you become a mother, you just learn that your life is no longer yours. All the best-laid plans go out the window. In some ways that was a rude awakening, but it was also like: get ready for the rollercoaster, man, because this is motherhood. You have no idea of the joy, the pain, the emotions, the absolute amazing feeling of being a mother. You do not know what that's like until that human being is right there and you realize you are not in control. I had this feeling of *Oh my God, what have I done? I'm responsible for this baby? For keeping it alive?* It was just this moment of complete fear and then also this feeling of *How am I going to do this as a working mom?* And there weren't many women in sports television who I could look to for advice, but I had this one friend who called me, and she didn't say, 'You're going to be fine, you're going to work it out.' Do you know what she said to me? She said, 'This is completely natural to feel this way. You're not alone.'

"It's funny. I always joked that if I was doing a story on motherhood, I would have read like 15 books, done all this prep. But I didn't do that for myself. I talked to my friends, and the only book I really had was the classic Dr. Spock [*Baby and Child Care*]. I was reading it and I get to the chapter where it talks about separation anxiety and how you shouldn't leave your child. I close the book, turn to my husband, and go, 'I'm not reading any more of this because this isn't applicable to me. That's not happening.' Traveling has always been a part of my job. You do miss your kids when you're away, but I remember my pediatrician saying to me, 'If you bring that baby on the road, that's about you. That's not about the baby. He's not learning anything. It's to make you feel good for—what—the hour you're going to be able to spend with him?' So when he was a baby, I only brought Will on the road with me one time, and that was for his first birthday during the Super Bowl.

"I missed a lot of birthdays. But what I learned is this: a birthday—like Christmas or any other holiday—it's just a date on the calendar. You can celebrate it on another day. You may not like it, but you adapt. I did have a seminal mommy moment that probably every working mother has had at one time or another. My son Will was maybe a year, a year and a half old, and I was getting ready to leave for a trip. He was clingy and he was never really like that. I felt his head, and it felt a little bit warm. I called the doctor, and he said to keep an eye on it. My car was outside, waiting to take me to the airport. And I'm looking at Will and thinking, *I can't go. I cannot leave.* So I called my boss and postponed my flight. I don't recall one scintilla of doubt that I did the right thing. Will didn't get sick thankfully, but he just wasn't feeling good and he wanted Mom around. I felt that tug, and that was the moment when I realized, *It's okay. Life will go on. I'm not going to lose my job. I need to be with my child.* And I encourage people to wait for that moment. We make so many sacrifices, and that shouldn't be one of them when you feel like your kid really, really needs you.

"I also had one of the worst experiences of my life on the road. I got pregnant again when my son was 22 months old. It was the end of the NFL regular season, and I was in the Bay Area shooting a story, and my phone rings. It was my doctor. He says, 'We got a bad amnio result...the baby is not viable. If you were to carry it to term, it would be stillborn or would die within minutes.' I literally fell to my knees crying. I was four-and-a-half months pregnant, alone, and away from home. I finished the shoot, flew home that night, and that's when I broke down. I walked in the door, and my husband didn't say one word to me; he just took my hand, walked me down the hallway, and opened up the door to Will's room, and we stood there and stared at him while he slept. My husband was basically saying, 'Look what we have. Look. What. We. Have.'

"You go through postpartum after a miscarriage, but there's no baby, and they don't warn you about that. They tell you about the physical stuff, but they don't really tell you about the mental stuff. And then on top of that, a few weeks later, I'm at the Super Bowl and I still look pregnant. Everyone is asking me, 'When are you due?' It was so brutal. Every day I would go back to my room and weep. It's still very fresh and traumatic for me, but I am extremely grateful for what I have.

Andrea's openness in sharing her pain hits so hard. But it doesn't surprise me that she's so willing to talk about it. That's just who she is! When Andrea and I started working together in 2006, she invited me to lunch so we could get to know each other. And right there, we made an unspoken pact, mother-to-mother, to support each other, to share stories, to share laughs, and to make sure we would never feel alone. That gesture meant the world to me, and we remain sisters-in-arms to this day. Through the years, Andrea has also mentored many journalists and broadcasters, including Jenn.

So, if you're lucky enough to find yourself an "Andrea," hang on to her. And if you have the chance to be that for someone else, do it! You never know how much it might mean.

—A.L.

"One of the greatest things about parenthood is coming up with your own little rituals, your own wonderful ways of doing things. When Will was a baby, and he'd wake up during the night to nurse, I would bring him into my bedroom, sit in a rocking chair, and nurse by candlelight. It was almost romantic—as long as you remembered to blow the candle out so you didn't set the house on fire. And whenever we had friends or family come over to the house, we would have them read Will a good night book before he went to bed. We'd take pictures of them doing it and then hang the pictures up on Will's wall. You and your partner are going to figure out your own ways of doing things. That's part of the fun, part of the enjoyment of it. There's no cookie cutter way to do anything. As a mom you come up with your own little things that are special and unique to your family.

"I had a child 3,000 miles away from home; I'm every mother's cautionary tale! But you have to trust the process. Even that first moment where I was giving birth a few days before the Super Bowl was a powerful moment for me. I got to experience the other side of what I always do. I always tell everybody else's story; now everybody wanted to tell mine. That was an eye-opener for me. It really informed me for the rest of my career how I would tell other people's stories. Because as a journalist, I may think I have a great story, but I have to remember, this is someone else's life. And as for motherhood? There is not one day in the world I have ever regretted becoming a mom."

13
HILARY AND WHITNEY PHELPS

AP Images

Whitney Phelps   Hilary Phelps

Meet Hilary and Whitney Phelps, part of the first family of swimming. You've probably seen them, along with their mom Debbie, cheering on their brother Michael. But long before he splashed onto the swimming scene, his older sisters had already made a name for themselves in the sport. Though their competitive swimming days are behind them, both sisters recognize that the "athlete mindset" still runs deep. Maybe that's what helps them celebrate the wins and, perhaps even more importantly, helps them get back on their feet when they fall—each in their own unique way. And in life outside the pool, well, it's no longer about winning. Sometimes, just knowing that you did your best is all you need.

In 2022 after 15 years of sobriety, Hilary decided to share her very personal story of addiction so that she could help others. She's embraced her path toward healing and, through her work as a speaker, advocate, and holistic wellness coach, she encourages others to do the same. Now divorced, she sees "having it all" more clearly than ever. Being present with her son Alexander brings her happiness and genuine joy.

I've learned that athletes are good at disassociating…in a healthy way. We can compartmentalize. One of the things that sports taught me is that I can get through anything. No matter how tough mentally and physically it may be, I know I can get through it. The mental component of sports is so helpful, especially now being a mom. Parenting is challenging and unpredictable, and so knowing I can do hard things, challenging things, helps on the days that are particularly rough. Same thing in recovery from addiction, too. One day might not be so good, but I've gotten through hard things in the past, so that helps me get through hard things in the present.

"As a collegiate athlete, I had to have structure, time management, goals, deadlines. I was a distance swimmer, so I swam before class. Now if I have to get all these things done with my child, well, that's where sports really helps. Like the other day we had a tight schedule—school, therapy, a quick dinner, and then we had to leave for baseball. We had time for five minutes on the playground, then home for bath and bed. Then there are the transition days, when a child of divorced parents has two homes, and they go from one to the next. Those can be really hard, and I try to be present and remember to focus on what my son needs at the moment and not what we had scheduled. We had one a couple of days ago. I picked Alexander up from school, and we were heading to a store. He was a little irritable. He wanted to go to a playground, so we did that first. He wanted me to chase him around, so I did that. Then, out of nowhere, he's like, 'Don't chase me!' I could just tell that he needed to talk. So, we sat there on this rock, and I just listened. He said he felt like I didn't love him. He was crying, I was crying. And I just listened to him. Then I looked at him and said, 'When I was little, I wanted to be a teacher and help children. Then I realized that the only thing I really wanted in life was to be a mom. When God gave me you, it was the best thing. He gave me *you*. I am so grateful to be *your* mom.'

"Alexander just looked at me and said, 'Really?' That was what he needed at that moment. Maybe that was what I needed, too. I forget to tell him sometimes how much I need him. We had that moment of connection and vulnerability and fear because he was showing up and being so honest, and I wanted to show up and be honest for him, too.

"When I became a mom, I had this idea of what my child would be. But I need to allow my son to be the person he is, and I have to adapt to that. As a mom I need to show up for him and not have him only show up for me. It's a hard lesson, but that moment in the playground was a beautiful teaching moment for me. I'm still learning how to show up in the world and, most importantly, how to show up for my child. I try not to get stuck in the super highs or the super lows either, but to exist somewhere in the middle, to appreciate and acknowledge things, and to keep going. My mom kind of had that tough love, which could have been a generational thing. For my brother and sister, that worked for them. And for me that approach did help me to succeed, but I was different. I got all the accolades for my performance in the pool, but I also wanted to be known as a good daughter and a good person. That informs my parenting now. I try to balance that. Like I'll say to Alexander, 'I saw you try so hard in swimming, but I also love the curiosity in your heart.' I don't know if that's going to work for him, but that's something that came from an awareness of my own needs.

This reminds me of conversations my sister Laura and I have. We were raised in the same household, by the same parents. Yet somehow, our experiences and what we each wanted was so different. I always wanted to be independent and she wanted more nurturing. And years later, we each brought our own perspectives into our parenting styles. Neither is right or wrong... it just is.

A.L.

"Can working moms have it all? What is 'all'? I think you have to define that first, and it changes all the time. Right now, I schedule my life in such a way that allows flexibility for playfulness and freedom with my child. That for me is success. Could I be making more money? Sure, but right now that's not what I consider success. I used to compare my life to some of the people around me and I'd feel like a failure, but then I realized none of that stuff—the big house, the cars—that doesn't matter to me right now. If we're in a two-bedroom apartment in Virginia, that's okay. We're happy. That to me right now is the definition of having it all. At the end of the day, it means being happy and joyful. That's much more important than any external validation any day.

"I joke that I'm the least successful swimmer in the family, which is funny because I got a full scholarship to a Division I school and broke all kinds of records. When my sister and other people started beating my time in the pool, I think some of that fed my addiction and also helped me seek help for it. My therapist helped me see that it's not all about the accolades and performance. Sometimes, it's just about knowing we did the best we could. That certainly applies to parenting.

"Like a few nights ago we had tuna for dinner. Some other days it's been peanut butter and jelly. Sometimes we have frozen waffles in the morning…not even homemade waffles. But I have had to get over that and remind myself that I did the best I could. My son's happy, fed, rested; I'm happy, fed, rested. Sometimes, that's enough. There's no such thing as a perfect parent. Like on social media, you see the five-course meal, the mom with the white dress, kids all dressed up. No, that's not real! As I've gotten older, I try to cut myself some slack. I'm gonna get up tomorrow, and it will be a better day. Life goes on. You have the choice to get up again and try again versus allowing it to sabotage everything else going on the rest of the week or whatever. Sports gave me that: the choice to get up and try again."

* * *

A few years younger than Hilary, Whitney Phelps initially had no desire to swim. But when she finally jumped in and won her first race, she was hooked. She began setting her own records in the pool and tried out for both the 1996 and 2000 Olympics. The latter, of course, was where her younger brother Michael made his Olympic debut. Although Whitney didn't qualify for the Olympics, that didn't stop her from competing at UNLV, where she quickly made her mark. But after an injury prevented her from continuing to swim, it became clear that life in Vegas was no longer right for her. Whitney made a very practical decision to return home to Baltimore and start a new chapter and career. And practical, well, that just seems to be Whitney's signature stroke.

"**A**s an athlete, I was always focused on being strong, mentally and physically. The workouts and training are insane! I remember when I was little trying to get out of going to swim practices. I was crying. I didn't want to swim. But then I won my first race, and that's when I fell in love with the sport. Swimming became my whole life, which was great—until it wasn't.

"When I went to school in Vegas, I ended up not graduating because I stopped swimming. And then everything kind of fell apart from there. I was like, *Oh, there's life outside of swimming.* I was bartending, and all that nightlife and all that crazy stuff. So, I came home to Maryland and started working in a manager training program, and that's where I met my now ex-husband.

"I stayed at home for six months when I had my first child, Taylor. She wouldn't go with anyone else. No one. My mom couldn't even hold her. If I left the room, Taylor would lose her mind. So, when I went back to work, I had to leave, and she had to learn to go to other people. She had to figure it out. I was like, *It'll be fine. She's not going to remember this. I'm not going to scar her for life.* I had to keep telling myself that. We just had to make it work. I have always been pretty practical through all the phases of my kids' lives. We as parents do what we need to do…and we make things work. I can't imagine not working. We grew up with a mom that was always working during the school year, and I had worked since I was 12. It was all I knew. I've always loved working and I love to provide for my family.

"But still, I'm constantly wondering: *Am I making the right decisions?* I think a lot of moms do that. Honestly, I just hope I'm doing everything right for the kids, making the right decisions, having them in the right places, and being a good role model for them. I hope to raise my kids to be resilient, kind, loving, and all-around good people. Obviously, nothing's going to be perfect, we all make mistakes, but I'm doing my best.

"At the same time—and this has taken a little while for me to understand—there are limits to what you can do and where you can be. You can't do it all, and it's really hard to ask for help. As I've gotten older, I realize it's not a weakness to ask for help; it's actually a strength. So now I ask! I've got my sisterhood, these five girls that are my people, and my fiancé Larry. They're the ones I lean on when I need help, or I'm feeling crazy or need to run something by them. No matter what, we have each other's backs and show up for each other. I can be so real and raw with them. I can be myself, and they love everything that comes with me as a person. And it's the same with them. There are days that I just don't know what I would do without them.

"Swimming was demanding, it was so regimented, scheduled, and predictable. And you just kind of had to handle things that came your way. So when I became a mom and had to balance so much, that wasn't new for me. You just figure it out. You adapt and you move on. You have to be strong for your kids and your family and all the people who need you.

"As an athlete, you're so results driven. But as a mom, it's not all about the results or about winning. You just have to do your best. I'm still competitive though! I was walking with Larry the other day and I had to walk faster than him and beat him. He said to me, 'It's not a race!' I know…it's nuts. But with the kids especially, I don't like to drop the ball or let them down. And sometimes I do have to miss things. Like the time my son Connor had regional finals for baseball, and my daughter Taylor had regionals for track. I had a meeting that I could not miss that day, so my hands were tied. I couldn't go to see either of my kids. Thankfully, their dad went to one, but that was really hard for me.

"And that's something that I say to other working moms: it's hard and stressful at times, but it's definitely doable. You figure it out. You may melt down on the way home from work or the way to work because you're overwhelmed and stressed. But now, I try to embrace all of it, embrace the craziness, and learn to roll with it. I mean, we're always busy now. I've got my two kids, Larry's kids—my three stepkids—and it's great. But the kids are going to grow, and they're not going to play sports all the time, and the schedule won't be as hectic. And when that happens, we'll have nothing but time."

14
HEATHER MITTS FEELEY

Heather Mitts Feeley has gone through a period of evolution and self-reflection that has taken her from gold medal-winning soccer player to full-time broadcaster and mom to a woman who is finally able to listen to her heart and spend more time at home with her husband and three children. Feeley has always been resilient on the soccer field, winning an NCAA championship with the University of Florida in 1998 and fighting through injuries to play professionally for over a decade and win a jaw-dropping three Olympic gold medals with the U.S. national team. But she has found a different type of resilience as a mom, one where she doesn't just bounce back from challenges, but springs forward...sometimes in a different direction. Feeley planned to stay home with her children—Connor (born in 2014), Blake (2016), and Ace (2018), but then the broadcast opportunities started coming; FIFA Women's World Cup coverage for FOX Sports, college football sideline and college soccer analyst roles with ESPN. Her broadcast partner at ESPN, play-by-play announcer Tom Hart, will share his thoughts on Feeley in this chapter as well. Heather and her husband, former NFL quarterback A.J. Feeley, balanced family and their busy working lives for years, but they also knew when it was time to make a change.

"**A**s an athlete, as a person, as a mother, I always want to do my best. When it came to motherhood, I was determined to figure it out and do everything that I could to succeed, including knowing when to ask for help. That's why I reached out to an expert when I was struggling. When it came to breastfeeding, I felt like I must have been doing something wrong with all of the pain that I was in. And it turns out, I was. It shouldn't hurt when your baby latches. I mean, of course it's going to hurt at first because your nipples are sensitive, and you aren't yet used to nursing. Nipple ointment, cabbage leaves, yes, they do really help. They can also ease the pain as long as you have the right latch. So, step one: get the latch right. Step two: figure out how to handle everything on the road.

"Oh my gosh, I think about all of the places that I've had to pump over the years. I pumped in airplanes, both in the bathroom [I'd put a sticky note on the door] and in my seat; in the back of an Uber ride [I had my cover on, but you could hear the pump slurping, and the driver was giving me the side-eye in the rearview mirror]; in a TV truck; a football coach's office. Honestly, that felt so weird. There I was in someone else's personal space with my boobs hanging out and my milk dripping. I think I would have rather pumped in a bathroom. The worst is when you're in there, taking care of business, and then you get these smells wafting in from another stall. It's seriously so disgusting, but you realize the lengths that we women go to as moms to provide for our children! It's just insane.

"I did some crazy things, too. I mean, mom brain, right? It's a real thing. I left my breast pump on a plane once. I also ended up leaving both my pump and my milk in Florida on one trip. And I was constantly trying to figure out what the best system was to store and transport my milk. Ice packs are great—they don't leak—but you have to figure out how to keep them frozen. Even if you do request an in-room refrigerator in your hotel, those little mini-fridges don't always have a proper freezer compartment. Regular ice? It works, but it needs to be replenished often and it leaks. I've left many a puddle of water and milk in the security bins at the airport.

"I even tried dry ice once. I packed it into my cooler with my milk, got on the plane, and tucked it under the seat in front of me. No problem. Yet when we started the descent, I heard someone say they saw smoke. That's when I looked up and realized that the smoke [or what looked like smoke] was coming from my cooler. Dry ice is actually a solid form of carbon dioxide—a little science lesson here that I learned the hard way—and changes in pressure or temperature like on an airplane can cause the dry ice to change from a solid to a gas. Hence the 'smoke' pouring from my bag.

"I definitely had some eyeballs on me. People probably thought I had some sort of bomb or weapon in there. Panicking, I tried to pick the bag up, but it was stuck to the floor. One of my milk bags had sprung a leak, and then the milk—thanks to the dry ice—froze to the floor. When I finally yanked the bag up, not only did I have smoke billowing, but I also had milk dripping all over the place. Double whammy! And would you believe I carried that thing—trailing smoke and dripping milk behind me—all through the airport to make my next connection? What a mess!

"Also ladies, hands-free bras and car adapters for your pump are a must because you're always running from one place to the next, so you might as well make use of that time. But let me tell you about my ingenious little invention. No need to pay extra for some fancy hands-free bra. Just take an old sports bra, cut some holes in the front, and put on your pump. *Voila*—pumping on the go! What can I say? It's efficient, and the pumping makes the time go by faster, too.

"Thinking back on those early years, I still remember how crazy and exhausting it all was. I think it was sheer determination that helped get me through. When I have something on my mind, I'm gonna do it. I'm not gonna give up. That's not who I am, and I really believe that's why I was able to have success on the soccer field and as a mom. But I want other women to realize that they are not alone. I think the one thing that most women don't tell one another ahead of time is how hard motherhood is—breastfeeding, especially. No one ever told me that. I didn't have any advice before I got into it myself and I would have liked to have known other women who had been there and heard their stories. Know that they had been through it, maybe get some tips and advice from them.

Heather's honesty, openness, and willingness to talk about her struggles certainly made us closer when we first started working together at ESPN. As someone who loved and followed women's soccer, I certainly knew of Heather, but I never imagined that one day she'd be pumping in the back of my rental car and telling me stories about areolas. It's true. Heather's night doula once advised her to "stuff your baby's entire mouth around your boob, including the areola." That word, right? I know. I'm pretty sure my eyebrows shot up in surprise, and my cheeks flushed with embarrassment when I heard Heather say it. But moments like that stripped away any distance I may have unconsciously put between us. So I certainly feel Heather's pain now when she tears up talking about her dad. He passed away in 2022, and that loss prompted some deep reflection on the type of woman and type of parent Heather really wanted to be.

—J.H.

"My dad worked his entire life as hard as he could to try to support his family and he was never able to take any time for himself, to go travel, or to do things he wanted to do…That taught me something. I thought, *I don't want that to be me. I want to be able to do the things that I enjoy, that are important to me, and that I love to do.* My mindset has changed a lot. Before I said yes to some things that maybe in retrospect I shouldn't have. Regardless, I think I learned from those experiences. But then later on down the road, I just said, *This isn't right for me and my family right now.* And I've been able to finally establish my boundaries. I never had boundaries before. I was never able to say no to anything. I think that's been huge for me as a person and also for my mental health, really getting to a place where I'm happy with what I'm trying to do overall.

"The hardest thing for me was trying to decide if I wanted to do both—work and be a mom—or if I just wanted to focus on being a mom. It's like I *can* be a working, successful mom and I *can* do all of this, but do I *want* to? That's what success means to a lot of people, but that may not be what success truly means to you. Everybody's success is different. You don't have to please anybody. You have to do what's right for you and for your family. If that means working full time, then that's amazing. I applaud all those women who work and have kids because I think that's the hardest juggle. But for me personally, I have also embraced the opportunity to take more time, not only for my family, but for myself. Moms take care of everybody else, but we come last when it comes to taking care of ourselves. It's important to do that because when you do, you become a better mom, a better wife, better at your job. You need to find the balance that works for you. It doesn't mean you're a failure if you make that choice not to work. It means you're doing what serves you the most. When you get to that place, then it becomes much easier to make the right decision for you. And you just don't look back.

"When I speak about the gold medal mindset, it speaks not only to my playing career, but also to how I approach life now. It's giving yourself permission to imagine a positive outcome. When we're adults, we have to continue to have dreams and goals to work toward. And you need to figure out who you are; that's taken me a long time, especially when I retired from playing soccer. It was like, *I was a soccer player before. So who am I now?* I am one Tough Mother. Mama Bear takes on a whole new meaning when you have your own. There's nothing like having your own kids, and when they're in this world, you just want to bring them up in the best way possible and make sure that you're loving them, supporting them, and encouraging them to be the best version of themselves. We're just here to help them to move in the right direction.

But I do believe there's something so special about being a mom. There's no better job in the world."

In our business we work with so many athletes and coaches with impressive resumes that it gets to be routine. Not to be rude, but it becomes somewhat irrelevant. You just want to know: can they do their job on air? When I first started working with Heather, I knew who she was, but when I looked her up, I was even more impressed. She's not intimidating, but her background is. Three Olympic gold medals? To have that level of training and discipline, to be an athlete at that level for that long is incredibly impressive. She's so friendly, fun, lighthearted, and good at her job. I thought, *What's next for her?* Motherhood, it turns out. And the juggling act that goes along with it.

Not that I had any clue just how much she was actually doing. I'm sure I could have been a lot more attentive than I was. But I'm a dude. When I get into a season, I have blinders on. I'd come home, and my wife would ask, "How's Heather doing?" And I'd say, "Uh, all I know is that Tennessee didn't score in the fourth quarter and lost the game." That's how my caveman brain works. So I wasn't aware and wasn't observant enough to notice that she was breastfeeding throughout that season. On our first or second weekend, we were in Gainesville, Florida. We had a Friday night dinner planned for the crew at one of my favorite sushi restaurants. We all piled into the car and drove over there, but Heather didn't get out. She said, "I'll catch up in a second."

I assumed she had to make a phone call or something. We got in the restaurant and started to order, and I realized she still was not there. I turned to our producer, Nick, who is a great guy and is obviously way more observant than I am, and asked, "Where's Heather?" He knew what was going on but was trying to keep it private. So he just said, "She's in the car." I kept asking him, "Is she okay? Do we need to check on her?" He finally looked at me and said, "She's pumping! She needs privacy." That's how clueless I was at the outset. But that's also when I first had the realization of all that she was trying to balance.

From then on, if she said she couldn't make dinner or needed to be late to a meeting, we just adjusted as best we could. Nobody thought twice about it. I'm a dad, and there were several other dads on our crew, and we just wanted to support her. My wife nursed all of our kids, and I remember how difficult it was at the beginning. Part of you never wants to meet your heroes because you're afraid they'll disappoint you. But Heather lived up to everything that I could have expected and more. She is awesome.

—Tom Hart, ESPN/SEC Network play-by-play announcer,
Feeley's 2014 broadcast partner

PART V
PASSION

—AIMEE

Those moments in sports when medals are won, when records are broken, and when all the training and sacrifice pays off—those are the moments when the passion of an athlete is undeniable. But despite being Olympians, competitors, and champions, the three Tough Mothers in this section—softball player Jessica Mendoza, swimmer Dara Torres, and long-distance runner Aliphine Tuliamuk—will tell you that their greatest passion lies in being a mother, a role they've fought hard to keep front and center.

When Jessica became a broadcaster and was told that to be the best in the booth she should keep her work and family separate, she brazenly ignored that advice. Then she doubled down on her decision, not only talking about her children with colleagues, but also frequently bringing them with her on the road. Dara will be quick to tell you that her daughter, Tessa, is "the reason I did everything." And Aliphine chose to have a baby between the U.S. Olympic trials and the Olympics. She made the team and then fought to bring her six-month-old breastfeeding daughter to Tokyo and in doing so helped start a movement.

Passion clearly runs deep in *all* of our Tough Mothers. Now, I'm not going to lie, sharing about myself in this section, well, that plays on all my insecurities. You see, for much of my life, I never really felt like I had that kind of passion. Working in sports for most of my career, I've seen what passion looks like at the highest level. It's filled with commitment and sacrifice; it's about wanting something so badly that you push through the pain and overcome the obstacles. But I never felt that strongly about anything I did while I was growing up.

I loved art classes and, since my dad was an artist, I had hoped that would give me an edge. When it quickly became clear that wasn't happening, I gave up. I didn't play any competitive sports in school. Despite the fact that my mom was 5'9" in the fifth grade, genetics didn't come to the rescue there either. I was small. So in middle school, I was that person who was picked last for dodgeball. I always exercised regularly, but unlike so many of the badass women in this book, I was quick to accept my limitations. I did long-distance cycling for a while, including a century ride, which was a brutal 103 miles. I had trained and was committed to doing those rides, but I didn't care at all about my time. In fact, when riders, who started after me, quickly passed me by, I stopped to cheer *them* on! So passion, it seemed, just wasn't my thing.

But that all changed once I became a working mom. Since then, I've pushed myself harder than I ever thought I could. I've overcome obstacles and I've met challenges from tough professional demands to finding unique ways to stay connected with my children while I was on the road for work. I've had exhausting commutes that often got me home too late to watch my kids' soccer games or to make it to the dinner table every night. Yet, as tired as I might have been, I pushed that aside when I walked in the door so we could enjoy a little family time before everyone went to bed. Those moments together were worth all the effort and the sacrifice.

Then it hit me—being a working mom is my passion! And I realized it drives everything that I do...and don't do. Like many of us working moms, I've had moments when I've questioned my ability to keep it all going. But my barometer was this—as long as my kids were doing okay, I was going to stick with it.

I knew they weren't going to be okay every moment of every day. As my son, Jay, likes to remind me: there was this one year that I was the only mom who didn't make it to Olympic Day. That's the Montebello Elementary School year-end tradition where kids compete in everything from potato sack races to the 40-yard dash. As Leone family legend has it, I warned Jay that I wasn't going to be there, but as he sprinted around the track, he saw a curly-haired woman in the stands. Thinking it was me, he ran over with such joy and excitement—only to be let down (and a bit embarrassed) when he found out that this imposter was not, in fact, his mom. That was tough for him, but it's behind us now (or so I thought until it came up again recently.) Through all of it, I've remained committed to making this family and career thing work...and I can't imagine my life without those two parts of me.

There have also been times when I've had to manage the judgment of others. Yeah, that's not easy. But for me facing it head on helped me realize that sometimes my harshest critic was none other than myself. I recall vividly a time I was dropping Jay off at his friend's house for a playdate. The mom is someone who I looked up to as the perfect mom. From the outside she made it look so easy. Her kids were always dressed beautifully, her house was spotless, and somehow she was always put together, too. On my best day, I was never able to achieve that trifecta of motherhood. I'm sure Jay's clothes were wrinkled and, knowing me, I was probably a few minutes late dropping him off. I assumed she thought I fell short because I was a working mom. Well, that day the two of us actually sat down and talked for hours about how hard motherhood is in general—whether you work or not. I was kind of in awe of her position, and as it turned out, she was of mine, and we began to better understand each other's struggles. I realized that she wasn't judging me the way I thought she was. My *own* feelings of guilt and inadequacy were getting in my way, and this honest conversation between two moms was just the reminder I needed to cut myself some slack and not judge myself—or others—for the choices we make.

So, yes, I'm *really* passionate about being a working mom. Everyone who knows me knows that (or as the kids say, IYKYK), and no one knows better than my husband, Wayne. I have chosen to devote myself to my family and to my work, and though other women may make different choices, the point is: that is our choice to make. Don't get me wrong; I am fully aware that staying home isn't an option for all moms. But, collectively, we as women do have more say in what our lives will look like compared to our grandmothers or even our mothers.

So for those of you who choose to stay home or for you mamas who gave work a try and realized that it wasn't for you, we know that you, too, are Tough Mothers. Whatever your situation is, don't doubt your own passion. It's there, burning inside you even if—like me—it might ignite you in a different kind of way. When you're following your heart, you'll know that's your passion leading the way. Or as Oprah Winfrey once said, "Passion is energy. Feel the passion that comes from focusing on what excites you."

15

JESSICA MENDOZA

Getty Images

As a softball player, television analyst, and mom, Jessica Mendoza has never been afraid to step into the batter's box. She was one of the very best to ever wield a bat for Stanford and for the U.S. national team. Mendoza was a four-time, first-team All-American, setting program records for batting average, hits, runs, and home runs. She is a two-time Olympian, winning gold and silver, and she's a member of the National Softball Hall of Fame. Mendoza began her television career in 2007 as a college football reporter and softball analyst, but she had her sights set on something no woman before her had ever done—calling baseball games as an analyst. And in 2015 Mendoza became the first woman to serve as an analyst for a nationally televised Major League Baseball game and she has gone on to fill the same role as a part of ESPN's Sunday Night Baseball *coverage and for the Los Angeles Dodgers. She is a proud mom of two boys, Caleb and Caden, and—rejecting some rather rotten advice she received early in her career—those boys have been on her lap and by her side through it all.*

"I get that feeling sometimes like, *Her kids are here again?* I don't want it to interfere with anyone else's job. So I ask my co-workers all the time if it's a problem. They're always saying, 'No, please bring the kids!' And I'm like, 'Don't tell me that unless you mean it because you know I will.'

"My kids will be a part of my work life. They've traveled with me—crazy as it was—for a long time. We made the decision to homeschool them so their schedule could be flexible enough to travel and so I could still be Mom even when I was on the road. I didn't really see a lot of other people bringing their kids. Even at the Little League World Series, I bring them every year and I got told by someone one year, 'Hey, maybe they shouldn't come the *whole* time.' I'm like, 'If you think it's affecting my work, we should have that conversation, but if you're just annoyed by the fact that my kids are still here, well, that's a different conversation.'

"People definitely have their opinions on it, but my work has always been a part of my kids' lives so they know who I am. When I was doing college football, I remember it was during bowl season, and it was so incredibly busy. I was doing three games in a row, I had to travel to all of them, and I had a three- or four-month-old at the time. He couldn't travel with me to those because it was just too much. So I had to tell my boss that I couldn't do all three games because I was still breastfeeding, and we didn't have enough milk at home. His response was to bring up another female reporter, one who at the time he felt was the best at her job. And he said, 'Do you know what makes her the best? She's a mom, but no one knows. She never talks about it.' So what he was saying was, 'If this is what you want to do, this is what makes the best the best.' Like basically just shut up about your mom problems. When I heard that, I thought, *Well then, I won't be the best.*

"In that moment I didn't think, 'Oh, shoot, I better stop telling people that I'm a mom.' It hurt, but to be honest, I remember thinking that if I'm going to do this, I have to do it my way. And I'm never going to hide the fact that I'm a mom. Both of my boys have been everywhere with me. There are tons of photos of them sitting in my lap during games, on air during broadcasts. I'll have a coloring packet in front of them, but it's still scary; you have this microphone, and if they say anything, it's live. But they've grown up with it. They've probably been to 15 different MLB stadiums. The World Series. Women's College World Series. Little League World

Series, they haven't missed one. When I was helping out the general manager of the Mets and I was in the front office, there we were with my kid sitting next to me, evaluating talent.

"I was eight months pregnant with both boys at the women's College World Series—they were both August babies—so they started out there in my belly. I remember being live on air at one Little League World Series, and we go to Julie Foudy, who is out on the hill in this cardboard box transportation contraption, and she's going down the hill, running people over. I look at the monitor, and there's my son with her driving that thing. My youngest, Caden, I've brought him to so many softball games. He wound up being the bat boy for my former team, Stanford. And it has changed his perception on female sports. He is my jock. But his dream is to play softball with the girls. He is obsessed. I just love that my 10-year-old would rather be at a women's sporting event than anywhere else in the world. I'm hanging on to that as long as I can.

"For me the pressure of doing live sports broadcasting taps into your at-bats. There's no asking the pitcher to throw a pitch again because you didn't really see it the first time. That's not gonna work. You have this moment and what are you going to do with it? I've found that most humans don't even want to be in the batter's box. They'd rather watch because it scares the shit out of them to be in such a big situation. So when I think about television, motherhood, all of it, it's something that I've craved my whole life. When I'm training at 5:00 AM or I'm doing things that are really hard, I'm doing it for the moment when the game is on the line. I want to be up to bat. I want to be the person in that moment. There have been times when I am really afraid, nervous, and wondering if I'm doing the right thing. My son is up all night and he's throwing up, and I've got to be at my best in the morning. *Can I do this? What am I doing? Why am I doing this?* And I have to remind myself if I had any choice in the world, I would choose this. I would choose these hard, pressure-packed moments.

"As an athlete I learned that. The best moments I've ever been in as an athlete were the ones that were scary, hard, and I didn't know the outcome. I knew I could totally screw up. But where else would I rather be? I have to remind myself of who I am. It's like being back in high school, a time when you're struggling to find your identity and confidence. I have had to retrain myself with that, to be honest, especially doing baseball. *Do I deserve to be here? I didn't play Major League Baseball. Should I be in this seat? Am I good enough?* I had to ask myself those questions because I do think those words of criticism from others hurt so much more when you believe there's even a bit of truth. If you have doubts and then some egghead on Twitter is saying something and it affects you, then there's probably something inside of you that believes it, too. So I've had to really search and ask, *Am I good enough to be here?* I don't want to be here because I'm a woman and we're checking a box. I definitely want to be here because I'm good. And when I am able to shout the answer as yes, that's when I can be my best.

"I had to practice that, practice believing in myself. It sounds silly to me to be 40 years old and telling myself to find that belief that I tell young girls to find, but I realized that I needed it. I had to really find out who I was. Once I did that, and I'm still constantly doing that, I try to pay attention to the things I do really well. Before, I was always finding the negative. But I switched the way that I did things, like 'Bring it on! Hate me, throw stuff at me, I've got a bat in my hand, I'll hit it!'

I don't care if you've ever played a sport in your life; that in a nutshell is an athlete's mindset. And that is also the mindset of a Tough Mother. You're going to put in the time as a parent and make mistakes, but you were made for this life of working motherhood. When those hard moments happen, when you feel uncertain about the outcome and the fear and doubt is creeping in, channel Jessica's inner voice and remind yourself—FUCK YES, I can do this!

—J.H.

"When I was doing college football and working in sports that are definitely not that supportive of working moms, I remember doing things like pumping in a broom closet in a football stadium 20 minutes before kickoff. I was struggling to get through games without leaking and I had already done one postgame report where I had leaked through my shirt and had to try and cover it up with my hair. I used to get pissed. Just by saying something like, 'I need to breastfeed,' it was like…when you're in school and you're on your period and you have to go to the bathroom? And the teacher's like, 'Shh! Zip it!' They were like, 'I don't want to hear about your personal business!' So I learned quickly: okay, I have to do this on my own. It's a lot. And it has challenged me. I think of when I was doing *Sunday Night Baseball* for ESPN, the level of intensity and seriousness throughout the week. There wasn't a day off. I had to do so much for one event. I think I had to compartmentalize to keep from crying because I just felt so overwhelmed. I would drive away from my house, and my now 14-year-old, who was probably eight at the time, would run all the way down the street chasing my car, barefoot in his cute little pajamas. I literally had to ask myself, *What am I doing?* I still think about that a lot, and it breaks my heart. And when I tell my son, he's like, 'I don't even remember that, Mom.'

That helps me now, and I share it with other moms who may be asking themselves that same question. But in those moments, which were years, it wasn't days; it's a blur. Two kids that were little, not having a day off, just the amount of stress, I don't regret it, but it was really, really hard.

"The No. 1 question I always get is: how do you balance it all? Sometimes I get annoyed because they don't ask the men that! I was doing an interview once with a baseball manager, and he pulled me aside and asked me about my kids, then said, 'Oh man, how do you do it? How do you leave them all the time?' And that phrase just hit me differently—like I left them on the side of the road, and they were hoping to get fed. I looked around his office and saw pictures of him with his children and I said, 'I'm here one day a week. You have 162 games. How do *you* do it?' He was like, 'Oh, well, it's different. I'm a man.' And I said, 'I don't see how it's different. You're a parent. If you can answer that question the same way you're asking it of me, then we can have a conversation.' And we just kind of got into it for a second. Part of it was my own defensiveness; it struck a chord. But I was sick of just taking it! And saying, 'Yeah, it's hard, I miss them so much.' I wanted to flip it and say, 'I'm sorry that you don't feel guilty that you're away from your kids, but I do feel guilty, and when you ask me that, it hurts. And so I'm going to turn it right back on you because I would hope that you care, too.'

"My husband, Adam, he's a stay-at-home dad. And he loves it. When we had our first child, I was working in television and playing on the national team. We were just coming off the Olympics, and there was a big decision by our whole crew that we really needed to try and help our professional league. I got offered a pro contract to go live in Florida. But I'm like, 'I can't go live in Florida! I have a newborn!' My husband was an engineer at the time, and we were trying to figure out how on Earth we were going to make this happen. So, I told the owner of the team that I needed a portion of my husband's salary to be covered, so that he could leave his job temporarily, and we could make this move. I thought for sure they'd give me the middle finger and say, 'Yeah, right,' but they didn't. They didn't skip a beat. They said yes. That was a life-changing decision for us. I probably never would have gone to Florida or made a lot of the choices that I did in my television career if this hadn't happened. What it allowed us to do was to really navigate this space of him not working, me playing at the time, and we all moved to Florida together. What was supposed to be a temporary decision is still our life now. My husband feels like his purpose on this Earth is to be a father, and it has been so beautiful to watch. He coaches all my sons' baseball teams. He's Super Dad. And then he supports me and is there for my career.

"He's an awesome human. The hardest thing is other people. Not so much now, but in the beginning, he would get asked all the time, 'What do you do for a living?' He sings it from the rooftops: 'I'm a stay-at-home dad!' He brags about it! For a long time, he'd get people who would respond, 'Okay but really, what do you do for a living?' He'd have to continually answer the question and get this skepticism of people wondering, *Well, what's wrong with you?* And it would bother him like, *Why can't the world understand this?* So I think that opened his eyes to see what I see in society almost in reverse as a man in this position. I'll also get it from women. That's the hardest: women on women. You feel like you're around your own kind of people, and then there's that judgment. You can tell. There are those little comments you hear from moms at school or women you work with who don't have kids, and they say stuff like, 'I would never choose that because I want to be a mom that's actually around.'

"My mom was a working mom, so I just thought being a mom is like…being a woman. It encompasses a lot of different things.

It was never a decision for me. I was going to be me. I'm going to have children, I'm going to be a mom, and I'm going to work. And we're going to figure that out. I had so many teammates that said they weren't going to play or work once they had kids like it was a decision you had to make and I didn't get that. I am respectful of whatever anyone else wants to do, but for me I'm going to keep on keeping on and I will have children. Everyone's path is their own. I want to encourage women to write their own story. You know deep down what you want to do; you can love your job, be passionate about what you're doing, and you are going to love the crap out of your children. Nothing is going to change that. And *you* know. No one else knows. So you do you, and forget about what society and anyone else has to say about it."

16
DARA TORRES

Most decorated U.S. female Olympic athlete of all time. Fastest female swimmer in American history. Oldest swimmer to ever make the Olympic team. Hall of Famer. Best-selling author. Motivational speaker. Coach. These are just some of the incredible titles that have belonged to five-time Olympic veteran Dara Torres at one time or another. But to her, none matter more than Mom. Torres had her daughter Tessa in 2006, two years before making her Olympic return as a 41 year old. Cue the inspiration for Torres' first book, Age is Just a Number. You'll get a chance to hear from Tessa herself, too, on what life has been like with her fit and famous mom. More humble and down to earth than you could ever imagine, Torres laughingly shows off her middle-of-the-day PJs while we chat. But she is also serious about her passion, and that's her daughter. This passion drives everything else in Torres' life, and she wants to make sure that no one ever forgets what stands alone atop her personal podium.

"**M**om should always be first. My daughter is always my No. 1. Sometimes I have to reiterate that to her because at times she thinks work comes first or this or that comes first, but she's my life. I would do anything for her. She's the reason why I did everything up to this point.

"When I decided that I wanted to make a comeback a little less than two years before the Olympics in 2008, there were a lot of questions that were going through my head. *Can I still be a great parent and be there for my daughter? Will my body hold up?* I really looked to working parents out there, both men and women, and tried to see how they balanced their workload with being a parent because you can still be a great parent if you're not there 24/7. So, I tried to work through my doubts, and then I was like, *Okay*, and I got rid of them. You can learn from your past, but don't dwell on your past. Look forward. That's always kind of been my motto.

"It is natural, though, to use some of what I've learned through swimming and apply that to other aspects of my life. There are a lot of parallels between being an athlete and being a parent. Coping mechanisms like time management, that is obviously super important with kids. Hard work, dedication, sacrifice. But I think for me it starts with passion, having a passion for something—for your sport, for your daughter—wanting to be happy with what you're doing and also making sure your daughter is happy with what she's doing. And that's really important. You have to feel good about yourself and what you're doing, whether it's to provide for your family or to do something that's going to make you happy that in turn will make your child happy. That's how you have to look at it. It doesn't mean you're not going to have guilt. That's normal! You're always going to have guilt when you're not with your kids. I know I did. I probably brought home a gift every time I was away, a little stuffed animal or something like that. So, there was a little bribery going on, too. [Authors' note: By the way, we fully support the small-scale bribery-to-ease-mom-guilt concept!]

"When I was home, I had to make up a schedule that would work best for both Tessa and me. I made sure I got up and did whatever I needed to do with her, then I went to my workout. I'd be there when she got home from school and then I went to practice. Kids are very routine-oriented. So if you get them in a routine, I think it makes it a little easier for them to understand what's going on. I also brought Tessa to the pool sometimes, so she could see what I would do as my work. That lasted like 20 minutes, and she was out! But I think it helps if kids understand what your work is, so that they can see what you do, and it sort of puts them at ease.

"Back then, USA Swimming had never had a mom on the national team—let alone an Olympic team. They had very strict rules, including no family in team hotels. Once I made the team in 2008, I knew I would be away for about six weeks between training and the Games. I got to see Tessa once during training camp, but even then I had to go to a different hotel to see her. So I decided to leave her home while I was in Beijing. That was tough. One of the things that I did was to make a calendar showing Tessa when I would be away. [Authors' note: Sound familiar? Mary Carillo did something like this too.] Every night before bed, she would X it off. She didn't really have a concept of time or how a calendar worked, but she could see the Xs leading up to the big star on the calendar that let her know when I'd be home.

"And I'll never forget when I got home from Beijing, it was late at night. The lady who had been watching Tessa left, and when Tessa woke up, I could hear her on the monitor. I walked in—just did a little 'psst, psst' because that was my thing that I did when I was there, and all of a sudden, Tessa jumps up and runs off the bed into my arms. It was literally the best feeling in the world. Even now, I leave sticky notes on the mirror each time that I have to leave for a trip. They just say, 'I love you, I miss you, have a good week,' things like that. I stick them on the mirror when Tessa is at school, so she'll see it when she gets home.

"I have had to travel a lot for work—I do motivational talks, too—and I say to Tessa, 'One day you'll understand why I do this. I'm saving for you! So you'll be taken care of.' And, of course, I'm not gone all the time. I have done a lot with her. I remember once when she got a little older, she said, 'Well, I never did gymnastics. And you were never at this...' And I pulled out the photo albums.

Here we are in gymnastics, there you are in dance, I'm taking this video at your dance recital. Sometimes you have to go back in time and show them that you were there because they have this thing in their head that because you travel and work that you were never there. I whip out that album a lot when she gives me any guilt.

Okay, I have to interject here because I had something similar happen recently with my daughter, Claire. Being the second child, she truly believes that her older brother, Jay, always got everything he wanted and that she didn't. I had the same complaint growing up, so maybe it's just a second-child thing. Anyway, Wayne just came across some childhood videos of Claire surrounded by toys, Claire splashing around in the pool laughing, and Claire running around the backyard with Jay. Both kids were filled with pure joy. Not at all in line with her narrative, so, of course, we had to share this evidence with her ASAP. We FaceTimed so she could watch it. After many smiles and laughs, she paused and said, "Wow, I guess I did have a good childhood after all!" Hmmm...imagine that!

—*A.L.*

"I actually gave *my* mom one of my gold medals. It was after Sydney [the 2000 Olympics]. I'd won three bronze and two golds and I wrapped it up as a Christmas gift. My mom was always giving me shit for keeping my medals under my bed. She was adamant that they had to be in a safe, in a bank, whatever. So, I gave it to her, and she was ecstatic! I just said, 'Listen: for all the years that you took me to my practices and my swim meets and have just been there for me, I want to give you this because you deserve this more than I do.' Then that summer I came out to see her and I walk in the house, and there's my gold medal in this big plexiglass case with light shining on it. And I'm like, 'Oh, so it's okay for *you* to have my medal out in plain sight!' But seriously, I should give her all of my medals for everything that she's done."

When I was younger, my mom traveled a lot. I would sometimes feel down about her not being there, but she always made sure to do something special for me. When I'd wake up in the morning, she'd leave a little note or a stuffed animal that she got for me. I still have the notes hanging up in my bathroom; they say things like "you're the best daughter," or "hope you have a great day," stuff like that. I dealt with a lot of bullying in middle school. I tend to stay in my shell, and not stand up for myself, but my mom taught me to be my own person. She is the toughest person I know, and she taught me to be tough. I'm super grateful for everything that she's done for me, and I'm very proud to have her as my mom.

—daughter Tessa at age 18

17
ALIPHINE TULIAMUK

AP Images

Aliphine Tuliamuk (all-FEEN TOOL-ya-MOOK) *is a long-distance runner and U.S. Olympian. Tuliamuk, who has 31 siblings, began running (often barefoot) in her native Kenya and eventually earned a track scholarship to come to the United States. She attended Iowa State and then Wichita State before graduating in 2013 as a 14-time All-American in track and field. Tuliamuk soon earned her U.S. citizenship and in 2020 won the U.S. Olympic marathon trials to qualify for the Tokyo Olympics. She and her husband, Tim, have a daughter, Zoe, born in 2021, the same year that the COVID-delayed Tokyo Olympics took place.*

"Choosing to have a child between the U.S. Olympic marathon trials and the Olympics, who does that? No one, to my knowledge. At least, not until me and Baby Zoe. There was so much riding on my victory, and I was so proud and excited to have earned a spot on the U.S. Olympic team for the Tokyo Games. I would become the first Black woman to represent the U.S. in an Olympic marathon. That race, the Olympic qualifying event, was held in February of 2020. As you know, things did not go exactly as planned after that. First, there was the COVID-19 pandemic, which pushed the 2020 Olympic Games back to 2021. And then there was me, thinking, *I do not really want to wait any more to have a family.* I have been given this extra year, so, I told my fiancé, Tim, 'Let's go for it!' In January of 2021—six months before the start of the rescheduled Olympic Games—out comes Baby Zoe! I know, I know. Who can do this? But to see her beautiful face and squeeze her chubby little arms, who is to deny me this grace? It was *my* choice, you see. And that is important. Tim and I were ready to start our family, and I was going to do whatever it took to be a great mother while also preparing for the biggest race of my life.

"Our bodies are amazing, right? To think that we can create a child, birth the child, and then produce milk to nourish that child—it really is incredible. Of course, we do not live in a vacuum, do we? We live in a world where we want to be a mother, yes, but we still want to be…whoever we were before we had a baby. For me, I was—and am still—a runner. When I went into my pregnancy, I was craving information. I wanted to know how other athletes at my level had gone through pregnancy and see how their story ended, see if they could come back to training. It would have been so valuable, hearing from those athletes, marathoners, to see how they handled things like breastfeeding and running. But that was not there. Some said they had to give up breastfeeding while training. I didn't want to do that. I was going to stop around four months, but my daughter, Zoe, she loved it. And actually I realized that I did, too. I was in a good place. I wanted to keep going. But how to do it? I was still producing a lot of milk even while training and I know I am fortunate in this respect. I was concerned, though, about the energy that it takes to produce milk and run at a high level. Honestly, I didn't know if I could do it.

"I took eight weeks off after giving birth, at least from running. I focused a lot on strengthening my core because I knew I would need it to be strong again to get me through my training. It was tough, but my best advice for new mothers coming back to exercise or train at an elite level is to take care of your body. That seems simple, I know. But it is your whole body that has gone through the trauma of childbirth. I know now that I needed more strength training not just in my core but in my hips and pelvic floor. It is not fun to focus on these things. Mornings when I would go for a run as a new mom, I would not feel like moving. I was so tired. I was wondering if I would ever run fast again. But if you continue to put in the work, your body will come back to normal. Your fitness will come back. You just need to take more time. Be kind to yourself. Know that you are not going to look the way you did before you got pregnant right away.

"One challenge for me was that my breasts almost tripled in size. They were so heavy. I went from wearing a small-size training bra pre-pregnancy to a large one, and that still wasn't enough. I would wear two bras. My chest was still so huge. I can't imagine how bad my form was. My breasts would be so full when I got home, and I couldn't even shower. I had to just rinse off and go breastfeed my child.

"For the first three months of my running, it was wake up around 5:00 AM, pump, breastfeed my child, pump again, and then run. That was a chore. I was not getting much sleep. But it was important to me, so I did it. Here's a thing about me: I'm very stubborn. I never really follow rules. I'm a rebel in that sense. I do what Aliphine wants to do most of the time, and Aliphine wanted to breastfeed and train! That stubbornness got me through a lot, I think. My training, it did get better. I got faster. About a month before the Olympics, we went to Atlanta for my first race back, and it actually went pretty well. I pumped and fed Zoe before I ran and I did fine. But the Olympic marathon? That was a whole different story.

"First of all, I had to fight to even be able to bring Zoe with me to Japan. Olympic organizers had made the decision due to the ongoing COVID-19 pandemic to not allow any friends or family members to travel to Tokyo with the athletes. And that included infants who were still breastfeeding. I could not believe it. I was so upset. I did try at first to accept the situation and I shared how I was feeling on Instagram. I wrote several posts on motherhood, including this one from June 27, 2021: 'I feel excited, but also torn…I know that I will be leaving [Zoe] for only 10 days, and she will be just fine, and that so many other moms have done the same, but I can't even imagine being away from her for half a day. My throat is lumpy. I know that everything I do is a teaching moment for her, I want her to know that even in the face of challenges that she can still follow her passion and prevail, now I need to tell this to myself, that even in the face of challenges like leaving my now 5 month old breast-feeding daughter behind for 10 days to race at the Olympics, I can prevail and show her how to be strong.'

"I was trying to tell myself these things, but I also had this strong feeling of just wrongness. And I was not the only one to feel this way. Other mother Olympians, like Canada's Kim Gaucher in basketball and U.S. Soccer's Alex Morgan, spoke up as well. Our anguish turned to outrage, especially as our story was picked up all over the world. And guess what? We got the Olympic organizers to reverse their decision! I'm really grateful that I could take my daughter with me. She was the only child that I saw there. When people saw Zoe, that put a smile on a lot of their faces. In that respect it was a great experience, and I'm glad that I didn't have to choose between going to Tokyo and quitting breastfeeding or staying home to take care of my daughter. I'm glad I pushed back. If there is a mom who wishes to continue to breastfeed and run, they should never have to choose between the two. That really lit a fire in me.

If, as the saying goes, "Hell hath no fury like a woman scorned," then a mother scorned transforms into an absolute firebrand. Aliphine helped to make change for breastfeeding mothers in Tokyo, and three years later in Paris, Allyson Felix partnered with Pampers to create the first-ever nursery at the Olympic village. Allyson, the most decorated female athlete in Olympic track and field history and a mother of two, has said she wants to be a voice for athlete moms. So now, Olympic athletes have a dedicated space to play with and care for their children, one less thing for them to worry about as they prepare for one of the biggest athletic events of their lives. As Aliphine can attest, though, life as a mother Olympian is still far from simple.

—J.H.

"My plan was to breastfeed at night, but travel, time changes, that has a way of messing things up. I had to sleep with Zoe in Tokyo. She had access to breastfeeding all night, and my breast tissue got really big. Then, the morning of the race—which, by the way, had to start an hour earlier because of the heat, so 6:00 AM instead of 7:00 AM—I almost missed breakfast. I had to wake up even earlier, and Zoe was not interested in feeding. I tried to pump, and nothing was coming out because I hadn't pumped much the last few days. So, I go to the start line—and I have my pump there with me because I know that I need to pump before I can run 26 miles—and there is no time left to pump! So there I am, ready to start the Olympic marathon with my breasts uncomfortably full. The one race that I needed to get everything right, I got everything wrong.

"And on top of that, I was also dealing with a hip injury that was more serious than I initially thought. I could not finish the race and had to drop out around halfway through. I was disappointed, of course. But also I felt proud. No, I did not win a medal, but I did have the opportunity to make life better for women who want to have babies and compete in the Olympics. I love being a mom. It's the most important thing in my life. Running can't compare to that. It's just my job. And I feel like I did win gold with my daughter."

PART VI
VULNERABILITY

—JENN

Who would have thought that vulnerability could be a strength? I'm not sure I ever thought of it that way until I heard from the Tough Mothers in this section. You'll read about my fellow ESPN broadcaster Tiffany Greene, who was brave enough to share her experience with postpartum depression. Rebecca Quin—you may know her as WWE superstar Becky Lynch—is the toughest of mothers, but she unveils a soft side you'd never see in the ring. And it's incredible how some of the most powerful women—like ESPNW head Susie Piotrkowski and Ally chief marketing officer Andrea Brimmer—admit to vulnerability being one of their most valuable assets.

Vulnerability can look different on all of us. We just have to start by lowering the shield that many of us have been holding up since we were girls. What we think is protecting us from the bad in the world could actually be isolating us from the good. When I was a kid playing kickball with the boys in the park, I would not allow myself to cry. I could have blood trickling down my leg from a scrape on my knee or feel the sharp tang from that stupid rubber ball after being pegged from close range and I would tell those tears to go right back where they came from. Because as a girl playing with the boys, I could not cry. That's what they all expected me to do. I won points on the respect scale every time I did something that they didn't expect—boot the ball over their heads into the outfield, beat them to a base, yell back at them if I disagreed with a rule—but crying? As Tom Hanks famously said in *A League of Their Own*, "There's no crying in baseball!" Or kickball, apparently.

Crying would drop me down to the very image I was trying so hard to defy—that of a weak, crybaby, never-should-have-let-her-play girl. I did not associate the word *girl* with weakness, but I knew that other people did. So I looked for every opportunity to prove them wrong. I still do actually. But I will tell you that my stance on crying has changed dramatically through motherhood, hormones, and maybe a better understanding of the power of vulnerability.

I cry all the damn time now. My kids will turn to me while we're watching a movie, notice the tears leaking from the corners of my eyes, and scold me, "MA-MA!" I suppose they understand when it's Jack sinking into the icy water in *Titanic*. But it's not just the big moments that get me. It's the moments of—I don't know— tenderness, which can occur just about anytime. Play that "Slipping Through My Fingers" mother/daughter scene from *Mamma Mia!*, and I'm a goner.

I'm more willing to show my emotions now, to be who I am, to feel what I feel, and to not worry about what others will think of me when I do. It's taken me some time to get here though. During the 2015 FIFA Women's World Cup in Canada, I absolutely lost it when my family left to go back home. My mom had come with me to help take care of my girls, who were eight and four at the time. My husband, Chris came, too, for a few days, but then when I still had about a week left in Canada, they all left. As I looked around my once-crowded hotel room, my chest heaved, my heartbeat quickened, and my body physically ratcheted up for the big, fat, ugly tears that were about to come. I plopped onto the sofa bed and broke down. I saw the painting my eight-year-old Ashley had made for me of lush, pink peonies, my favorite flower. I remembered the slap of cards on the kitchen table, my four-year-old Maddie telling me to "Go Fish" when I asked for the Poky Little Puppy, the Tawny Scrawny Lion, the Saggy Baggy Elephant, or some other Little Golden Books character on the cards. My two sweet girls were nowhere near me yet everywhere around me at the same time.

Moments like this are all-encompassing. You feel your pain, doubt, guilt, all of these crippling emotions in every molecule of your body. There is no easy way out of that. And I know that at the time what intensified my misery was that I felt I could not show this side of myself to anyone else. I was the only female play-by-play announcer for FOX at this World Cup, the only *girl* in that role. And here I was on the school playground once again, fearing that I could not show my colleagues how hard it was for me to be away from my children. I wish I could have had an Andrea Brimmer or Susie Piotrkowski in my life then to tell me that it was in fact okay to feel all of those things, that it didn't make me any less of a professional, that in fact it illuminated me as a whole human being rather than just a broadcaster.

We all, as working mothers, have to decide for ourselves how much we reveal of who we really are and how much we admit to the struggles that wrap themselves around us every day. The choice is not to be vulnerable or not. We have included vulnerability as a Tough Mother Tenet because it's essential. Acknowledging your soft spots can actually give you strength. How much vulnerability you show the rest of the world at any given moment is entirely up to you.

18
REBECCA QUIN
(aka BECKY LYNCH)

Rebecca Quin—aka Becky Lynch, aka "The Man"—is a WWE super-star and eight-time world champion who has transformed women's wrestling forever. She became the first ever SmackDown women's champion and the first woman to win the main event at WrestleMania.

She was also the first woman to step away from the WWE—at the height of her career—and return as a mother. Quin and her husband, Colby Lopez (aka WWE superstar Seth Rollins), welcomed daughter Roux into the world in December of 2020. Since then, Quin has gone on to win more championships and write a best-selling book, all while struggling with the conflict and guilt we working moms know well. Quin is proof that even the toughest of mothers, those who blaze trails and break barriers, need strength and reas-surance, too.

"I find that I struggle with…all of it. Being a mother, especially when you're in a predominantly male-dominated industry where the top guys don't have to leave to go have a child, it challenges you. But I wanted a kid. I knew I wanted to have a family. And then immediately I started wondering, *Have I ruined my career? I worked my entire life to get this career.* And these are not the questions that you should be worrying about. It should be a thing where: yes, you're able to have a kid, here are the concessions that we can make to help you because that's part of life. I remember mostly support coming in, but there were some negative responses, and I wanted to prove those people wrong while also proving to myself that I didn't have to sacrifice one for the other.

"Then you have a kid, and you're on the road 52 weeks a year, and it's difficult. You're constantly grappling with the guilt. It's so different watching the male brain versus the female brain, too. My husband is wonderful, he's the most incredible father and partner, but no part of him feels like he should give up his career to be a dad. But there is that instinct in me and I imagine in a lot of women. And I'm like, *What is all of this guilt?* Because I watched my mom. She was a flight attendant and she was the predominant breadwinner in my house. I always looked at her and thought, *What a badass! She's doing all this, she's holding it down, she's working, she's coming back home and making cakes for the bake sale. She's there, she's involved.* But she was also gone, and I never held that against her. I only ever revered that about her. But then when it's me in it and I'm looking at it from the other side, I feel like I'm gone too much. It's this constant worry, and I'm continually finding things to beat myself up about. I'm constantly wondering, *Am I scarring my child, am I doing this all right?* [Authors' note: These fears are so universal, but as Rebecca is brought to tears sharing them, it's clear they also feel so deeply personal.]

"With wrestling you learn to not be so attached to anything. Sometimes, we'll get an idea for what we're doing for a show, and then two hours before we go live, it will all change. You have to learn to go with the flow and be willing to adapt and adjust on the fly. That is motherhood. You have all these images of yourself before you have a kid: my kid is never going to eat sugar or watch TV, they're going to be quiet and sit there and play with their toys, and everything will be perfect and pristine. And then you realize it is not even slightly like that. You throw out all of your preconceived notions and make room for something even better. That's the biggest thing that I've learned: not being attached to anything and being flexible. You can't dwell on your mistakes. You learn and move on.

"As far as being a mom and wrestling, I suppose it's a matter of just doing it, being a crash test dummy, and proving it can be done. And it's not like I was the first mother in wrestling. There were women who had kids and then they came to WWE. But as far as I know, before me nobody had left at the top of their game as champion, had a kid, and then came back to work a full-time schedule. But then when someone goes and has a baby and their career isn't over, you realize, *Oh, okay, this can be done. It's not that big of a deal. We actually can have it all.*

"I've just never felt like I should have to accept less because of my gender. I grew up in Ireland, and we had a female president, and my mom was the primary breadwinner in our household. But I also remember I went to a Catholic church, and only boys could serve at the altar. Then they finally let girls be altar girls, and I was like, 'Hell yeah, let me get in there.' Whenever there is a chance for change, we should be in there! When I'd watch wrestling as a kid, I'd wonder *Why are women relegated to being in their underwear and their whole value is decided upon their appearance? What is this bullshit?* There are girls who can wrestle. Just let them wrestle. We are not just our bodies, we are not just our faces, we are human beings. It would always upset me that women just weren't treated equally. I couldn't accept that I couldn't be seen in the same vein as Stone Cold Steve Austin, The Rock, or Mick Foley because I was born a woman. That made no sense to me. There was always kind of a rage against the machine of being valued based on a male's perception of how we look. I just couldn't accept that. I wanted to change it.

"'The Man' originated because I was rising through the ranks from underdog to one of the top stars, and in our industry and many others, the top person is usually called 'The Man.' I was 'The Man!' I was claiming that moniker for myself. And it worked.

"So I had this whole tough-guy, bad-ass persona, and then when I got pregnant, I wondered if I would be perceived as less of a bad ass as a mother. I wanted to flip that perception on its head and change the narrative. I've always had that desire to turn the narrative. 'Why can't I do this? Because I'm a woman you're saying I can't Main Event WrestleMania? Well, I'll prove you wrong. You're saying because I'm a woman I have to choose between having a career and having a family? Well, I'll prove you wrong.'

"I'm extremely proud of being a mother. But I also worried that my whole identification would become that I'm a mom as opposed to I'm an athlete and I'm also a mom. Motherhood is another layer of who I am. Your whole identity and purpose shifts when you become a mom because now there's something far more important than just you and your goals. You've got to look after this child, this little person who relies on you. They need you, and you need to craft them into a decent member of society.

"But for me holding on to the person that I was and the job that I do was so important. It's part of who I am, too, and we do do need to hold onto that part of ourselves. I have to remember and constantly remind myself that it's okay to want to excel in my career because one day my daughter may be faced with the same dilemmas and I just have to be that model for her. It doesn't need to be one or the other; you can have both.

"That's being 'The Man.' It's taking care of your family. It's having your priorities in order, but also not making yourself a martyr... and allowing yourself the joy and the fulfillment that comes from chasing your dreams and doing what you love.

Yes, you're damn right it's okay to want to excel in your career *and* try to be the best parent and role model. After all, that's why we're here with you...to remind you that you can do this. So if you're questioning that right now, we hope it gives you some comfort knowing that even 'The Man,' Becky Lynch, feels your pain. There's this whole if-you-can see-it, you-can-be-it initiative going on right now, so allow yourself that fulfillment and let your kids see what's possible.

–A.L.

"A lot of women in wrestling have now had kids and come back, and it's been awesome to see. I'm sure we all still struggle with those questions of: *Is it possible? Are we going to be judged? Are we going to be defined by this?* And the answer is no. I mean, the answer is maybe yes to some people, but, eh, fuck 'em."

19

ANDREA BRIMMER

On the one hand, Andrea Brimmer, chief marketing and public relations officer at Ally Financial, is this incredibly fierce and awe-inspiring woman in a position of power. But Brimmer is also a mother who struggles with guilt and challenges like the rest of us and she wants you to see that side, too. Although not all of us have a boss who gets up and walks out of meetings to go to her kid's hockey games and encourages her employees to do the same, we can all benefit from seeing what a world run by enlightened women (and men) can look like. Brimmer and her team, many of whom are women, moms, and former athletes, have been a big part of her trailblazing push to invest in and amplify women's sports. Brimmer's children, who are now grown, are well aware of their mother's success, but as you'll hear, they are even more grateful for the role she has played in their lives.

Brimmer believes in supporting women, especially working women, even though she grew up with a mother who stayed at home. But that mother, Hilda, has always been a fierce advocate of women's rights. She went to Gloria Steinem rallies and was a card-carrying member of NOW (the National Organization of Women). And when Andrea wanted to go back to work after having kids, Hilda had her back. That steadfast support has been vital to Andrea throughout her life but particularly in one horrific encounter. This powerful businesswoman, who rolls into board-rooms proudly flashing her "Like a Girl" tattoo, also understands the value of vulnerability. She opens up here about a moment that changed who she is and how she approaches life and working motherhood.

"I was scared to tell my boss I was pregnant. Keep in mind it was the late 1990s, and I was working at an advertising agency in charge of one of the biggest pieces of business that we had. I'd had trouble getting pregnant with my first kid and then unexpectedly got pregnant again pretty quickly. So I had been promoted and I knew I was pregnant and I was starting to show. My boss was on the 10th floor—I remember this so clearly because it was such a terrible experience—and I was on the ninth floor. So I went upstairs to tell him, and he was like, 'Ohhhhh, that's good. Congratulations, I'm happy for you.' We talked about how long I'd be on leave, and I said the usual stuff all us women do: 'Don't worry, we'll figure it out. I'll be back as fast as I can,' even though I was going to have two kids under the age of two. So, it was all fine, and then when I was leaving, he asked if I was walking back down to my office. I said I was. He then said: 'Hopefully, you'll fall down the stairs. Ha, just kidding!'

"I will never forget that. That's when I became so determined never to quit on womankind. I will never make someone feel like that, no matter what job I'm in. And I want to show women that it's okay. Have your baby. Take this time with your child because it's the most precious time in the world. I had a lot of complications with Drew, my second child. I unexpectedly went into labor 10 weeks early. I was in the hospital on bed rest, and my boss—yes, this same boss—called me and chewed me out because I didn't have any transition plans. I mean, I didn't expect to go into labor 10 weeks early! He called me in the hospital and made me feel just awful. And I remember my mom—because she was there with me—taking the phone out of my hand, and she was like, 'I am Andrea's mom. This woman is in pretty bad condition, the baby's in critical condition. How *dare* you call my daughter, who has given you her heart and soul for all these years, and let her have it for not having a transition plan? I have a mind to drive down there and take care of you myself.'

"I did come back to that job, and it was hard. I had two kids under two, a big job, and I know there were a lot of people at the agency hoping I would fail. Mostly men. But I didn't! It was very traumatic, but it was very life-changing for me, not only in terms of how long I would continue to be employed there—because I knew I had to leave—but also in how I would show up for other women.

"Throughout a lot of my kids' childhood—for about 13 years—I was a single mom. Their father and I divorced, and I didn't add my second family—my husband, Mark, and my amazing bonus kids, as I call them, Samantha and Peyton—until many years later. I do think strong women need strong men who are also not afraid of a woman's power or a woman's success, and Mark has been that for me. He has given me the support system that I needed both emotionally and physically to show up the way that I need to show up at work. But back then it was just me. I had these two little boys and I wanted them to see why I wasn't around. I was the primary breadwinner, and it was important for me to take them everywhere that I could. I took them to conferences and let them see me speak. I'd take them to New York, and they got super used to the city. I would bring them to all kinds of events, and they were always my 'spouse.' Everyone knew it was just Andrea and the boys. It just made us so close. And it also really made them appreciate the demands that I had. I love and am very purposeful in talking about my kids at work. I see a lot of women hiding that side of them. Don't hide it! It's what makes you you... and it's going to make your kids better, too.

"I remember this one time my son Alec was in fourth grade, and I went with him to something at school. The neighborhood we lived in, it was all stay-at-home moms. So I show up in head-to-toe black Prada and I don't look like anyone else. Alec grabs me by the hand, walks me right up to his teacher, and says, 'This is my mom, and she's not like the other moms.' He recognized it and he was proud of it. I believe really good women raise really good men. And the more really good men we've got in this world, the better we're gonna be. My boys both realize the importance of showing up for your partner to give them not only support, but also space if they need it. I see how they are in their relationships and I know that stems from what they witnessed with me, how I showed up for them, what I instilled in them, and insisted was important to them as men. When the kids were younger and had to write papers on the person they admired most, they chose me. They talked about the way that I showed up for them, and Alec, my oldest, will say to this day, 'We knew my mom had a big job, but we also knew that any minute we needed her—she could be in a board meeting or whatever—but if we called her and said we needed her, she was walking out and she was going to be there for us.'

"And that means the most to me of anything.

"I used to have the mom guilt thing bad and I overcompensated by buying the kids stuff. When Alec was 16, I bought him his first car, this little sports car. And my ex was like, 'What are you doing?' But it was the mom guilt! It was super dumb. No 16-year-old kid needs that kind of a car. It took a couple of years of that, and then I realized—guilt is a useless emotion. I think that really hit me when I saw the kids write those papers about me. There was nothing in there about what I bought them or about me not being there for them. It was all about, 'I'm so proud of my mom and the way she shows up for me.' It freed me. It's like it took chains off my heart that were so heavy.

I carried that mom guilt around for years, too, for the times I was away on business trips, for those moments I missed when I was at work, and for all those things I can't even remember. But later it was my kids who told me to let it go. They assured me that all the times I was there for them are what meant the most. As for me being away from them when I prepared for the Olympics—my kids were like 'Mom, let it go. We don't even remember that stuff you struggled with. We remember going to the Olympics!' Hearing that from them took those heavy chains off *my* heart. When you're in the thick of it, sometimes you just need that reassurance that you're doing okay.

—A.L.

"Alec was a big jock. He played hockey, and his senior year, I made a promise to him that I wouldn't miss any of his games. And hockey has like 1,000 games! Okay, I think the season was like 35 games. But no matter where I was in the country, if I had to get up in the middle of a meeting to catch a flight to his game, I did it. We had this really cool thing, where I knew he was waiting for me. And I'd get there sometimes just in the nick of time and I could see him on the ice just looking for me in the stands. He'd come over to the glass and he'd tap his stick the minute he saw me. And every time he scored or had a good play, he'd tap his stick and point at me. He knew I'd made him that promise to be there.

"The secondary effect of that for the women on my team was that they'd see me get up and leave. And I made no bones about it. 'Hey, guys, I'm sorry. I'm going to my son's hockey game.' And it showed them that was okay. You've got to get up and go? Go. You need to leave because you promised your kid you'd be at something? Good for you. Go do it. If the boss is doing it, then it sure damn well is okay for you to do it.

"Being in such male-dominated industries for so long and hearing things like, 'Oh, you hit the golf ball like a girl' or 'You throw like a girl' or 'You do this like a girl,' it bothered me. There were nights that I didn't want to go out and party with all the guys by myself because I knew the inherent dangers of it. If anything were to happen, of course it would come back on me. So I'd go back to my room early and they'd be like, *Don't be a girl.*

"I wanted to take the power back somehow like, *You're damn right I'm a girl!* And getting a tattoo with the words 'Like a Girl' was my way of doing that, showing the world I do everything like a girl. I kick like a girl. You want to feel what that feels like? Come on over here. I run like a girl. I love like a girl. I work like a girl. And it's a beautiful, powerful thing. So the tattoo was a public statement to the world. And there are times, I'll be honest with you, when I'm in a room full of guys and I'll purposely put my arm up so they can see it, like *This signal's for you, bro.* But also for me, I wanted the tattoo where it is because I see it all the time. It's a reminder to not ever forget what my mantra is. I truly believe that people are put on this Earth to do things, and one of the things I was put on this Earth to do was to show other women a path to how things can be done.

"I've always taken on more responsibility than my age or tenure would tell you I should. It's always been a part of my natural ethos for whatever reason. When I played soccer in high school, I played varsity as a freshman, and as a sophomore, they made me captain, even though there were a bunch of seniors on the team. For whatever reason I think I've got that I-want-to-lead mentality. And when I got into the workplace—I started working in the advertising industry in the late '80s—there was still a dress code for women. We had to wear nylons, skirts—swear to God—every single day. So I would go to the advertising agency in a skirt and a perky bow and a blouse and a jacket and nylons. It was all men. I didn't look up and see any women. I was always the only woman in the room. And at a very early age, I noticed it. It drove me to make change, but it also made me mad. *Where are all the women?* The only thing that my boss—that same jerk boss—ever said that was insightful was this: I asked him one day, 'How come I'm the only woman in a leadership position?' He said, 'We'd love to have more women in leadership positions, but they just never stay.' Part of me was like, *Well, that's because you're a jerk, and you don't make them feel welcome, so they decide to leave.* But the other part was like, *There's probably a lot of women who think this is just too hard and they can't do it, and somebody's got to show them that they can.*

"That's when I came up with this idea that life is sloppy, and it's okay. You've got to embrace the slop. Sometimes I'm going to be a great mom; other times I'm going to be a really crappy mom. And sometimes I'm going to be a great employee, and other times I'm going to be distracted and not so good. And sometimes I need to be selfish and show up for myself and go on that girls weekend or I need to go to the spa or I need to leave in the middle of the day and go for a run because I'm not going to be any good for anybody if I don't. When I finally embraced that, that I can't be perfect all the time, it was so empowering. And I felt I needed to demonstrate that for others. I think as women we feel like we always have to be perfect, always. That was a big unlock for me, and I wanted to show other women that it's okay. I started talking very publicly about the slop. I've been talking about it for years and years. And you can see, especially in young women, the relief in their faces when they're like, 'Wow. She's sloppy, too? Thank God! I can be sloppy!' [Authors' note: Andrea references the slop in a letter she wrote to her former self for her alma mater, Michigan State, in which she says she purposely made herself very vulnerable.]

"You have to be honest about what you're going through. When you're younger, you're more guarded. You want everyone to think you're Teflon. We all think we can jump off a building and be fine when we're in our 20s. Then life throws a couple of hard knocks at you. When I was a single mom, that was probably the darkest time of my life. I was in a really bad, toxic relationship. My brother was dying from MS. I had two little kids. My family was a mess. My parents were an absolute mess; they hated the guy I was dating. He wasn't allowed in their house. They weren't speaking to me. Talk about being alone; I could not have been more alone. That was the hardest time of my life, and I wanted to share that with people. Because if people, especially women, know that I went through that and came out the other end, then they know they can go through almost anything and come out the other end, too. So many students reached out to me in response to the letter, particularly female students, and they said, 'Thank you so much for being honest. We didn't expect this. It meant so much because this is what I'm struggling with.'

"And I'm really vulnerable with my kids, too, like, 'I went through what you're going through. It's okay.' I think sometimes, especially my older two, they feel this incredible amount of pressure to be a CMO or CEO and I'm like, 'You don't! Just enjoy your job and enjoy your ride. Before I got this job, I screwed a lot of stuff up. Trust me.' So I think vulnerability is critical. I don't think you can be the best version of yourself unless you're honest about the things you're not good at or the things that you have struggled with. Going back to work—or not—after having kids is a very personal decision, and you can't make a wrong choice. Some women say they want to stay home and take care of their kids, and that's okay. Others say, 'No, my career is really important to me. I want to come back.' And the biggest thing I tell those women is: 'Make sure that you have the right infrastructure around you. Don't collapse under the weight of it. It's okay to get a nanny or whatever choice you make for the help you need. Get the support system you need because you being strong and mentally fit and physically fit to be able to take on what you're going to take on is the biggest gift that you can give your kids.'"

I grew up playing hockey, and hockey moms always had a reputation of being some bad-ass women, but my mom took being a hockey mom to an entirely different level. There was one game I specifically remember where I was playing incredibly well and had three goals in the first period. During the second period, one of the dads from the opposing team yelled, "Someone take out No. 7's knees." My mom is just 5'3", but she absolutely went after this guy. She yelled, "What the hell did you just say?" And then: "If you have a problem, you can meet me in the parking lot." Thank God the other hockey moms were there to restrain her, or else that man would've had it coming. After the game he actually apologized to my mom for his comments. The reason I love that story is that it shows my mom's tenacity and willingness to fight for her children. It doesn't matter who you are or how big you are. If you say something about her kids, she is going to defend them and she would go to war for us. She already knows this, but she is my superhero, and I'm so fortunate to have her. She had to make a lot of sacrifices for my brother and I while we were growing up, and at the time, we might have been confused, but it all makes sense now, and I wouldn't change a thing about it. I love her more than she will ever know.

—son Alec at age 26

One thing that I admire the most about my mom is her selflessness. Every day she wakes up and exemplifies what it means to be a strong, independent woman, but she has remained remarkably selfless. She checks in on all of her kids every single day. Whether it's solving our daily problems, offering advice, or simply telling us she is proud of us, she never skips a beat. If you call her, she will be there to lend a hand. One time we met a nice man at a local bar who spent the whole night raving about his love for the Daytona 500 but noted he had never been able to attend a race. Without saying a word to anyone, my mother stepped outside, made a few phone calls, and got the man VIP passes to the Daytona 500. Acts of selflessness like this happen almost daily, and I couldn't be more appreciative. My mom has taught me to help others whenever you have the power and ability to do so.

—bonus daughter Samantha at age 25

I used to be much more shy than other boys my age and always wanted to play with dolls and dresses instead of action figures and cars. Unfortunately, I suffered a lot of bullying from peers and even family members because of this. My mom, however, did not make me feel ashamed of this. One of my fondest memories with her was going to the nail salon together and getting my thumb painted blue. (I was too scared to get all my fingers painted.) I remember how elated I was in the moment to feel like I could be myself without judgment from anybody and I knew that my mom would have my back if somebody did say something. As time went on, I learned that my mom faced a lot of backlash from certain family members and other parents for allowing me to express myself how I wanted. She never backed down in the face of so much negativity, though, and made sure I was the happiest child I could be. Now as an openly gay adult, I know that I can be—and should be—proud of who I am. Although there were many times I missed her growing up and wished she could stay home, every moment with her was and is filled with joy and laughter. Being away from each other was that much more bearable knowing that the time we would spend together would be so wonderful.

—son Drew at age 24

20
TIFFANY GREENE

Tiffany Greene is a groundbreaking play-by-play commentator for ESPN. She is the first Black woman to do play by play for college football on a major network and in 2021 received the Dawn Staley Excellence in Broadcasting Award. She is one of the main faces and voices of ESPN's HBCU (Historically Black Colleges and Universities) coverage and she herself is a fourth generation Florida A&M Rattler. While in school Greene earned a degree in broadcast journalism and was a member of the Rattlers bowling team. She has long known that she wanted to be a sports broadcaster, but she also always knew that she wanted to be a mom. Tiffany and her husband, Aaron, have two sons—Bryson born in 2017 and Aaron "Deuce" born in 2020. But Greene's first few weeks of motherhood weren't exactly what she had envisioned. Her honesty and openness about her journey shines a light on something that so many moms, working or not, often go through privately, and Greene's mother-in-law, Lo Berry, shares her valuable insight as well.

"**P**ostpartum depression. There. I said it. Yes, I had it. And it was scary as all get out.

"I am the type of person who always wanted a family, but I definitely took my time in getting there. I was working my way up in sports broadcasting and I had big dreams. I have called all kinds of sports, including basketball, softball, volleyball, and yeah—fist bump for all the ladies working in this man's world—even football. It's just crazy how things work, though, because the truth is it takes a lot of work, and I knew I needed time to focus on that before I started a family.

"So in 2016 my husband, Aaron, and I decided we were ready to give it a go. I got pregnant, and we were fired up! I tried to stay in the know and was always searching for info on what to do and how to do it while I was pregnant. You can drive yourself crazy with all of this information gathering, but I just wanted to be prepared.

"Not that I felt at all prepared when the baby actually got here. Our first son, Bryson, was born in March of 2017. I figured I would give breastfeeding a try. Man, I was so optimistic and excited and… naive. I had no idea what I was getting myself into. Knowing what I know now and having gone through what I did, I liken breastfeeding to straight up hazing. For real. I was like, *I already went through the entire pledge process. I did that in college. I do not need to do that again.* It would have been real easy to whip up some formula, but I did not want to be told that I couldn't do something. That's where, I think, all of my trouble began.

"My pediatrician was recommended to me by a friend. She was a young woman like me. She was pretty matter of fact. Not that that really means anything, but I'm just trying to paint you a picture. My husband and I took Bryson to his first check-up after we left the hospital, and the doctor asked me if I was breastfeeding. I said that I was. She said pretty bluntly that Bryson was not getting enough to eat. She told me that if he didn't gain more weight in three days, when we came back for our next appointment, then I was going to have to put him on formula. I was reeling. I was like, *Don't you know I'm just here trying to handle all of this right now?* That wasn't even a jab. It was like a combo body shot/uppercut. Then, to make matters worse, she brings my husband into the mix. We had been worrying about how much Bryson was getting to eat, but when the doctor said what she said, Aaron hit me with an I-told-you-so look and said, 'See?' In that moment I was like, *Did you just violate all of our wedding vows? You're trying to prove a point to me now with this doctor attacking me and you don't have my back?* I took that so personally. I was just triggered. And you know what I felt? What word kept pounding and pounding in my head? *Failure.* Here I was, busting my butt doing everything I thought I should be doing, and it wasn't working. I was feeling guilty because I had all this support and I understand not everyone has that. So why was I being such a big baby? Why couldn't I suck it up and keep going?

"I had a lactation consultant, a doula [a woman who comes in to provide guidance and support to new parents], my husband, my family. My mother-in-law even runs a business that helps new mothers. So in my eyes I had a charmed situation. And I was still, as I felt, failing. That made me beat myself up. And you know, as a new mom, I was also tired as all get out.

"In my head I was asking, *How do I rid myself of these problems?* There is one part of the equation that could make everything go away and be better. I mean, you hear that now, and your eyes just go wide with shock, right? I know. I never really thought that I would do anything to harm my baby in real life, but subconsciously in my dreams I thought otherwise. And it scared the bejeezus out of me.

Tiffany is so incredibly brave to share this story. I didn't experience any post-partum depression, at least not to this extent. But if I did, I wonder, *Would I have been brave enough to tell people about it? To face the judgment? To admit that I, as a mother, even subconsciously had thoughts of harming my child?* I wince every time I think about it. And then I think of all of the women who have felt this way and how we need to embrace them and support them and I'm so grateful for people like Tiffany.

—*J.H.*

"I can remember this one time so clearly. I was laying down on our daybed in our downstairs bedroom office. I put on some sort of Soundscapes relaxation music with sounds of the ocean and closed my eyes. I thought, *I am finally relaxing. It's quiet. I feel like I'm in a deep sleep and I'm getting rest. I long for this rest.* And that's when your subconscious kicks in. I felt the words bubbling up into my mind. *How can I maintain this rest? The ocean is so vast and deep, peaceful, tranquil. If I just lay the baby in there, he can just float off in peace. We can both be at peace.* That was my exact thought. That I now know is postpartum depression. It is scary and it is real.

"My husband already knew that something wasn't quite right with me. I was lashing out, and he took the brunt of it. I'm sure he felt beat up on a little bit because I was critical of a lot of things, just real short with my temper, definitely not showing the love that he was showing back to me. My tank was empty.

"So when I came to Aaron and told him about my dream, he sounded the alarm. My mother-in-law, Lo, called me. She helped talk me through my feelings and got us set up with a postpartum doula. I never knew about doulas until about 30 weeks into my pregnancy. No lie, my birth and postpartum doulas—women who come in and help with whatever you need—helped to change the course of my life. We had a social worker come to our house. There's this whole testing process, where you have to answer questions and they come back multiple times. Understandably, they want to see what kind of a state you as parents are in. We talked about the pressures of parenthood and how I didn't need to feel like I was doing it all on my own. They reminded me that the stress of caring for a baby and the baby itself are two different things. It's not the baby's fault. Sometimes, even though you know it in your heart, you just need to hear somebody say that. We worked together and got through it. I started feeling like myself again. I still had my challenges, but we did it. *We* did it. Not just me and Bryson, but me and my husband and my doula and my parents and in-laws. You may feel like you're in it alone, but you're not. Never forget that. If I learned anything, it's that you've got to let those people in your world help you however they can. Let them fill you up when your tank gets empty."

As a mother I couldn't ask for a better spouse for my son than Tiffany. I hoped he'd find his soulmate, and he did. Tiffany is giving and sharing, always willing to impart knowledge and support. She knows how to be a friend. She reaches out to assist other people and she puts her mark on peoples' minds and hearts. I remember vividly what she went through after having her first son. This is an area that I've been working in for 20 years, addressing maternal health, particularly for African American women and women of color. Just about the time that Tiffany opened up and really talked about it with me, I was on the cusp of asking her about how she was feeling and how I could help. I noticed some of the symptoms, and there was definitely a difference in her mood and attitude. She's very upbeat, very active, and usually in good spirits. I saw her feeling and looking depressed. She was experiencing some shame and guilt about what she believed wasn't being successful with breastfeeding.

She started feeling and appearing panicky much more than what we were accustomed to. Making decisions usually seemed to be pretty easy for her, but I noticed that even small decisions became a task. Then there was the exhaustion. Almost every time I went over there, and I was there almost every day, she was exhausted, and her stress level was definitely elevated.

One thing I recommended was that she consider using a postpartum doula. We were actually doing a pilot study with them for my company, and so I signed Tiffany up as well. The postpartum doula is quite different from a labor and birth doula, who are there to help only for the first few weeks. A postpartum doula can step in later and lend support with whatever the family needs—washing dishes, helping to straighten up the house, holding the baby at the worst hours so that the mother can sleep. It's just someone to be there and lend support.

That was quite helpful for Tiffany. It gave her time to rest and it also gave her somebody to talk to about what she was going through. Postpartum depression affects one in seven women who give birth in the U.S. On top of that there's anxiety and depression, and that affects about one in five women, and 800,000 new parents a year experience maternal mental health issues.

Nobody knows your body and you better than you. Assert yourself. If something doesn't feel right, doesn't seem right, then it's probably not. Your mental status and your physical well-being are important. It's not all about the baby. I would also say to make sure that you have a connection with strong partners. Do not do birth and delivery and the period that follows in isolation. Whether that is a spouse, significant other, your best friend—just make sure you have that support system in place to share this journey with you.

Finally, make sure you go to your postpartum visit. That's where you can get help, not only for your baby, but also for you. If something is not right, your doctor may be able to help you pinpoint what is going on and have suggestions on what you can do to feel better. I saw Tiffany go from sheer panic to a level of comfort. I've seen her go from a lack of trust in her ability to be a good mom to getting a good handle on things. I couldn't be more proud of her, and her boys absolutely adore her.

—Estrellita "Lo" Berry, Tiffany Greene's mother-in-law and founder of

REACHUP, Inc., a non-profit that promotes and protects the health of

pregnant women, their infants, and young children

21

SUSIE PIOTRKOWSKI

There are certain people you come across in life that just make you think, I want to follow them. Susie Piotrkowski is one of those people. As the vice president of women's sports programming and espnW at ESPN, she is in charge of the development, execution, and creation of ESPN's women sports strategy and female audience expansion efforts. She has that it factor. You can feel her strength and drive pulsing through every word she says, but Piotrkowski's greatest strength may lie in her ability to be vulnerable and honest with herself and those around her. She can do that because she feels seen and supported for exactly who she is.

I am a queer woman. I am a mom. I am in a high-profile position at ESPN, where I focus on the growth, development, and coverage of women's sports. I take all of that very seriously. As a queer woman, I often think about how I can best champion the full LGBTQ+ community because I sit in a position of tremendous privilege. I need to make sure I am a voice that everyone can be proud of. I want to make sure that everyone knows that I have a wife, that we have a daughter. I ask pronouns. The way I see it, my job is to be a bridge builder to help people become more open-minded both in my work and as a human more generally.

"When my wife and I got married, we knew that for some people attending our wedding, this might be the only gay wedding that they'd go to. So we took on the responsibility of showing them that our love is no different than anyone else's love. We are a two-mom family and we view that as a tremendous opportunity to represent our community. We talk openly about how our familial structure is different and we try to be very intentional about how we spend our time. We prioritize time in therapy. We look at it as maintenance, as something that can help us be better parents and partners.

"It's also really important to us for our daughter, Rew, to see two working moms, to show her what that actually means. I have a really demanding job. I have to be on the road a lot, but I also set boundaries. And my wife, Brittany, keeps me honest with that. She knows how important my work is as well as what type of mom I want to be to our daughter. She makes sure I always keep the main thing the main thing.

"Communication and intentionality. That is what makes my world work, and I know it is informed by having been an athlete. Setting a game plan, being intentional with my time, being well-prepared. I thoroughly believe in what I believe. I speak up about it, and that, too, comes from the confidence built as an athlete. As a working mom, you've probably been asked—or maybe have even asked yourself—about 'having it all' and if that's really possible. But who defines what 'all of it' is? I'm a very full version of myself right now in my life. I am full. I am vibing. Do I feel proud of how I show up as a mom? Yeah. Do I feel proud of how I show up at work? Yeah. Do I feel proud of how I show up with my wife and with my family? Yeah. Are they all equal all of the time? Absolutely not. They're varying. Each doesn't carry the same weight at the same time on the same day.

"When I go on vacation, I'm not looking at my shit. I really am not. I have to be intentional about that because that's what I need to be 100 percent for my family right then. With my job I'm not 100 percent for my family, but you can be well-balanced…enough. Everyone's sense of full is different. There are times when I have to make sacrifices at work to show up for my family or times that I have to take a little off my plate with what I do at home. And that's okay. I've learned to love and accept that about myself and I also know it is okay because of the amazing people and privilege I have around me, and not everyone has those options. I think we define what 'all of it' is. When we try to prescribe to these more antiquated perspectives that oftentimes have been defined by men for women, we lose. When we define it for ourselves, I feel like we're closer to winning.

This absolutely blows me away. What an incredible perspective! To hear Susie talk about "having it all" in this way is so invigorating and inspiring. I'm ready to stamp that shit on a pencil or motivational sticker right now. I know I have wrestled with that notion of having it all plenty of times. In fact, I got into a pretty heated discussion with my book club about this very topic a few months ago. (Yes, I know. I fully own my suburban dorkiness by talking about my book club.) One of the other working moms in our group posed that question: "Can we really have it all?" And she followed it somewhat heart-breakingly with: "I'm not really sure that we can." I almost lost my mind. I passionately defended the notion that yes, we can have it all. I feel like this is the premise that I base my entire existence on. Hearing Susie's perspective is so incredibly validating.

–J.H.

"I wanted a career in sports, but if you had asked me in the beginning, I probably would have told you that I'd be doing something in men's sports. But after several years in the business, I was having a bit of an existential crisis, asking myself if what I was doing aligned with who I was and who I wanted to be. I realized, to put it bluntly, that I didn't only want to make rich White men richer. We work for a large portion of our lives, and I have always wanted my work to feed my soul. So I bet the house on women's sports. And now I can't fathom working in anything else. At ESPN I get to help build a sustainable infrastructure alongside so many who have been working towards this foundational shift in the landscape for decades that will support the women's sports ecosystem not just today—but ideally for generations of women and athletes to come.

"Vulnerability is so important. But to truly be vulnerable, you need to feel supported. I have a friend, Jess Smith [president of the WNBA Golden State Valkyries] who's a mom to two girls, and one is exactly my daughter's age. I can't tell you how often we go to each other not only for general career advice, but also for those moments when we may be struggling as parents or partners. I'll be like, 'Do you feel like you're letting your whole family down right now?' And she's like, 'Yeah, do you feel like you're letting your whole family down right now?' I don't know what I would do without another working mom who is in a very similar position to me because she validates me. I don't feel as alone. I never feel judged by her. Honestly, having that kind of support in my life is what allows me to be vulnerable."

PART VII
FOCUS

—AIMEE

Working in sports, I see the athletes' focus just about every day. If you're a sports fan, I'm sure you know what it looks like. It's just who they are. It's what's separated them from others for most of their lives. But you don't have to be an athlete to have it. Each of the moms in the pages that follow focus on the prize, the goal, the positive, and the progress.

You will feel the pain of ESPN broadcaster Laura Rutledge as she gets patted down in an airport security line while her bottles of breast milk sit warming outside their cooler. You will sense the intense focus from World Cup champion Alex Morgan as she continues her fight to make the playing field more equitable for women often with her daughter Charlie attached to her hip. And you will see, through the words of North Carolina women's basketball coach Courtney Banghart, that even the strongest of us can be derailed by doubt unless we find a way to shift our focus for the better.

I have a tattoo of an arrow on my wrist to remind me to focus forward, to not dwell on the past or the things I can't change but to learn from them and to keep moving. I'm a planner, always have been. I guess that means I focus on getting things done. But that wasn't so easy when Wayne and I decided to start a family. We had some challenges and we had to pivot and take another approach—fertility pills. My doctor knew from my history that I probably wasn't going to get pregnant any other way, but he was fairly optimistic that one or two rounds of fertility pills would do the trick. So even though we were disappointed and scared, his optimism helped alleviate our concerns. I know that I was lucky. I have friends who had to go through extensive treatments and I'm sure some of you mamas reading this may have experienced that, too. But, hopefully, the fact that you're here with us now means that you found your path to motherhood one way or another.

Our bump on the road to pregnancy just made me more focused on making it happen. I was working at a production company in New York called No Sleep Productions (fitting, I suppose, for a soon-to-be mother). One of the shows I worked on was *LATER...with Bob Costas*. Costas was going to host the Olympics in Barcelona the following summer, so I knew our show would be off the air during that time. What that meant for me was that I had a window of opportunity. If I could have a baby in May or June, I wouldn't have to miss that much work and I could plan my maternity leave while the show was on hiatus during the Olympics. I know this sounds absolutely nuts, but being the ultimate planner, maybe bordering on control freak, I thought I could make it work.

This was the early '90s, and we didn't have any fertility apps or cell phone calendar reminders back then. So I had to figure out on my own how to make the timing work. I tracked everything. I had my calendar book with all of my private notes. I counted back 40 or so weeks from my preferred due date, figured out when I'd take the pills, and I locked in a strict cutoff date, a kind of go/no go approach. If I could get pregnant within that time frame, great. If not, we might have to pause on activating the launch sequence (a nod to my favorite line from *Everybody Loves Raymond*). And then on one of those make-it-happen-NOW days on my calendar, I had to take a last-minute business trip to Los Angeles, but with my laser focus, I knew what needed to be done. Wayne booked a last-minute flight to join me in L.A. After all, I had already taken my fertility pills, and... well, you can figure out the rest.

Lo and behold, nine months later, with Costas on his way to Barcelona and a repeat episode of *LATER* on the television in the delivery room, I gave one last push, and my son Jay was born. It was the ultimate coup in planning and control, and to this day, I still can't believe it worked that way. My focus shifted pretty quickly to preparing for life as a working mom. Wayne had just started his own business. So even before I got pregnant, we had both agreed that I would go back to work. I was completely on board because I loved my job—and still do—and honestly, was grateful I wouldn't have to wrestle with that decision as a new mom. And once we made that our plan, no one was going to tell me I couldn't do it. Not the doubters. Not the laundry commercials featuring stay-at-home moms and all the subliminal messages about what a mom was supposed to be at the time. Not the woman who couldn't hold back her judgment and said, "I'm not going back to work because *I* choose to raise my *own* kids." Yes, someone actually said that to me. I hope she knows that she made me even more determined to show that I could do it. And if I ever need a reminder, there's that tattoo on my wrist to redirect my focus. Because after all, the harder you pull back on an arrow, the farther forward it flies.

22

LAURA RUTLEDGE

Laura Rutledge joined ESPN in 2014, and since then her star has continued to rise. Rutledge is a sideline reporter for some of the network's biggest events, including the Super Bowl and the College Football Playoff. If you're an SEC fan, you no doubt know Rutledge from her days hosting SEC Network's weekly, on-campus tailgating show, SEC Nation. *In 2020 Rutledge also became the host of ESPN's daily weekday show,* NFL Live, *and in 2024 she added hosting* Welcome to the Masters *to her already impressive resume. She absolutely is as kind, genuine, smart, and funny as she comes across on television. She and her husband, Josh, have two children: Reese born in 2019 (and famous in her own right for her helmet game day picks) and Jack born in 2023. Rutledge shares her life as a working mom because she wants to lead other women to believe that they, too, can follow their dreams and start a family.*

There were so many times when I started in this career of sports television that I thought there was no way that I could have children and be in this business. Not only has that been proven wrong, but my career has actually grown exponentially since I've had these children, which is something that is truly beyond my wildest dreams. I am trying really hard to show the positives of what this life can be. And while certainly there are so many challenges, I think if women see other women doing it, it makes it more palatable and attainable to them, and that really matters to me. It is possible to have all of this: to have a full-time career and to be a mom and a wife.

"Now, that being said, I will share some of my struggles with you here. I usually hesitate to talk or post much about the hard stuff because I always feel like at the end of the day I've been incredibly blessed to do what I'm doing and to have this job. I feel for single moms working multiple jobs to make ends meet and I feel like, *Golly, my struggles—while they're valid and they happen every single day—they are just not at the level of what some of these other moms are going through.* Still, the timing of my first child—smack dab in the middle of college football season—did pose some challenges. My husband Josh and I had been trying to get pregnant for a while, and I had all but given up when all of a sudden—boom—baby in the belly! I had a lot of worry. I thought, *This is literally the worst possible time.* What you don't realize is that when you have a child, it's the best time at any time.

"That's me trying to live in a world of gratitude, something that I work at every day, but I'll be honest, when I had my first child, Reese, I was crazy. I mean, I can see that now. I was desperately trying to prove that this whole mothering thing was no big deal, or maybe that wasn't quite it exactly. I knew it was a big deal. I mean, I had no clue how hard it would actually be, but I think, as working women, there is a certain need to prove that motherhood is just another task that we can handle, right? In some ways that's exactly what I did. Three weeks after giving birth, I was back at work and back on the road, hosting *SEC Nation.* But here's what you might not know and what I really want you—*need* you—to know. It about broke me. I may have looked like I was ready, but I wasn't. There is nothing, and I mean nothing that can prepare you for that feeling of leaving your baby for the first time. I remember sitting on the plane, tears streaming down my face, thinking, *What am I doing?* But also at the same time, I felt that pull of wanting to get back to work, to have that semblance of normalcy, to prove that I could do it.

"I wound up exclusively pumping for both of my babies; we just could not get the latch to work for breastfeeding. And on that first trip, I had to pump on the floor of a family bathroom in the Atlanta airport. Underneath the toilet was an outlet, so I had my face next to the toilet, and there I was, pumping before my flight. Ugh! That took some focus. That experience, though, was just the warm-up for what came next. Week Two I was in Jacksonville, Florida, for the annual Georgia–Florida game. I was feeling pretty good like, *I've got this figured out!* Turns out, no. No, I did not. At 11:00 PM the night before the *SEC Nation* show, I'm in an Uber trying to get to a pharmacy to get medicine. Why? Well, I had mastitis. Technically, mastitis is inflammation of the breast tissue, but it hits your whole body. It's very painful, and you feel really sick, or at least I did. I called my doctor, who told me I was going to end up in the hospital if I didn't take care of it immediately. I hadn't told anyone other than my family what I was dealing with, but I still wanted to do the show. It was my decision. So I got the medicine, still felt pretty miserable, and did the show like a crazy person!

"After that whole ordeal, I was ready to go home. I went to the airport in Jacksonville, where, while going through security, the TSA agents took out every single bag of breast milk that I had with me. Fine, I get it; I know that's part of the deal. But while they have all of my milk sitting there outside of the cooler, they also decide that they need to take a closer look at me. They start doing these massive tests, including opening up my pants because my giant, extra-absorbent postpartum diaper is somehow setting off an alarm. This is all happening in front of my co-workers, by the way. The TSA agents did pull me aside to try and provide some semblance of privacy when they asked me to unzip my pants, but I was so embarrassed. I needed to pump. I was still in pain from the mastitis. My milk was sitting there, getting warm. And I thought, *Why am I doing this? Why am I putting myself through this, going through this embarrassment, and piling on so much more stress?* I really grappled with whether I should continue breastfeeding at that point.

Wow, I watched Laura on TV during this time and couldn't believe how together she looked so soon after the birth of her first child. Her anecdote is a reminder that things are *never* what they appear to be. Laura was facing many of the same challenges the rest of us do, trying to balance it all. But she has this public-facing job, so she was determined to keep going, stay focused, and never let us see her sweat! I'm sure some of you can relate. We kiss our babies goodbye, wipe the baby drool off our shoulder, and we switch into work mode without missing a beat.

Then there are those times where it just doesn't go to plan. Like the day that my my husband Wayne had to be at work early, so I was solo that morning. I got our son Jay ready for school, got myself ready for work, and was giving our daughter Claire her favorite cereal for breakfast. The morning routine was going perfectly. I was on track to make the 8:19 train to the city, which would get me into the office just in time for my morning meeting. But as I was about to leave her with the babysitter, Claire threw a wrench—actually a Cheerio—into that plan! She stuck some cereal up her nose, and as I said good-bye, she sniffed and had a look of terror when she realized it was lodged in there somewhere. I'm embarrassed to say that I was a little angry at first, so I took a deep breath and had to just be mom at that moment. She was so scared as I put a tweezer up her nostril to carefully remove it. She ended up being fine, I missed the meeting, and 20-plus years later, that story remains one of the family favorites.

—A.L.

"I have learned that you have to be able to laugh at yourself in some of your more desperate and ridiculous moments. I had a very, let's say, unforgettable, run-in with one of ESPN's tech support guys when I was trying to do radio from home. During the COVID-19 pandemic, we started doing more work remotely, which as a new mom was fine by me. I had a studio set up in my home, and I had this great plan. I thought, *I'm going to do radio, pump while doing it, and hope that my pump is quiet enough to where I don't have to explain myself.* So I get going, get hooked up, think everything is good to go, and then they're like, 'Well, there's no Internet connection.' I'm wrapped up in my pump cords with the pump tubes and the power cord and then I've also got the radio headset, ethernet cords—all these cords! I am trying to stay connected to the wall but also get these cords straightened out; it's this whole mess. Things are falling over, I'm knocking things over, all of that. Then the I.T. guy says, 'Can I just FaceTime you right now? That way, I'll be able to explain all of this a little better.' And I'm like, 'Yeah, you probably don't want to FaceTime me right now.' I mean, what am I supposed to say at that point? I just went with the truth and said, 'I have my shirt off and I'm pumping milk!' Just this terribly awkward moment with this person that I do not know at 5:30 in the morning.

"Nobody has it all figured out. Anybody who makes you feel like they do, they don't! We're all just day to day, trying to find different ways to make things work, and the way that it works for me may not be the way that it works for somebody else. So many times we're forcing a round peg into a square hole because we're thinking, *Oh, I have to do it how this other person did it because that must be the only right way.* The judgment zone should just not exist! I hate that it does, and I think we all deal with that. That's where a lot of the mom guilt comes from, and I feel that every second of every day. I've discovered that it compounds on itself, too. You think, *Okay, the way that I'm going to fix this is by doing more. I'm going to exert more of myself.* Instead of just being there and being present, you're trying to do too much. And then it gets worse and worse because then you feel like you're failing at what you're doing and you feel guilty about that on top of everything else.

"There was a weekend not long ago where I had been out of town, and Josh had been working and at home with the kids, and I knew he needed a break. So I said, 'Why don't you go golf? I've got this.' Well, of course, that means I'm pumping and chasing the one-year-old around while connected to the pump. Reese is causing all sorts of havoc because she thinks that she's the mom and she's trying to pick Jack up and carry him all over the place. He was about to go down the stairs because he figured out how to open up the baby gate, and I'm running, still with the pump attached, and the milk is spilling everywhere. I was like, *This is so bad!* Then, when I try to clean up, baby Jack is into my husband's new set of golf clubs—that we're not supposed to touch—banging them on the ground, banging himself on the head. And I'm thinking, *Okay, this is a disaster!* I probably should have told Josh, 'You know what? Just give me a chance to pump and then you can leave.' But I didn't because I was trying to be like, 'No, I've got it.' I felt guilty about not being there, and that's something that I've been trying to identify before it gets the best of me. I have to ask myself, *Okay, are you doing too much? Are you really capable of handling all of this?*

"When you're living in this world of high-functioning anxiety all the time—and a lot of us working moms are—we're feeling like, *I'm okay, but I am feeling kind of anxious and I might fall over, but it's okay.* Then, all of a sudden, it catches up to you. And you find that manifesting in a variety of ways. I am notorious for that. So trying to stop that train before it rolls down the tracks has been a little bit of a challenge for me, especially since adding a second child into the mix. I remember when I had just come back to work and I was trying to juggle everything and I felt like I was just falling short in all aspects, and my friend and colleague, Elle Duncan, who is a mom of two, gave me some great advice. She said, 'Hey, here is what I ask myself about my kids every day: are they loved and are they safe? If those two things are true, then you're good.' There have been so many times where I've started to feel myself get overwhelmed, and I've taken a moment to say, *Okay, but they are loved and they are safe. They might have a cold, they might be upset, I might feel like I'm not giving enough of myself to them—whatever it is—but at the end of the day, they are 100 percent loved and 100 percent safe.* That really helped keep me focused on what matters. It's a beautiful mess, this working mom life, but it's something that I'm very thankful for."

23
ALEX MORGAN

Getty Images

The image of Alex Morgan has changed a lot since she stampeded onto the international stage at the FIFA Women's World Cup in 2011. At the time, the 22-year-old, nicknamed "Baby Horse" for her long, galloping strides, was a lightning-quick goal scorer who would soon become one of the faces of the U.S. national team. Morgan led the Americans to Olympic gold in 2012 and winning back-to-back World Cups in 2015 and 2019. While Morgan was building her soccer career, she was also growing her own personal brand, appearing in everything from Sports Illustrated *swimsuit edition covers, to Maroon 5 music videos, to a seemingly endless stream of endorsements and business ventures. More recently, she co-founded the media company TOGETHXR and created the Alex Morgan Foundation, both of which are female-focused. Morgan has consistently been at the forefront of change. When a group of players sued U.S. Soccer for equal pay in 2016, Morgan's name was on the actual EEOC (Equal Employment Opportunity Commission) charge of discrimination: "Alex Morgan et al. v. United States Soccer Federation, Inc." The suit was settled in 2022, and Morgan stood proudly on Audi Field in Washington, D.C., signing the historic new collective bargaining agreement with her two-year-old daughter, Charlie, nestled in her arms. Morgan's life has changed as a working/playing mom, but her focus remains razor sharp.*

"**M**y life as a working mom is busy, it's chaotic, but it's also something that I love and enjoy so much. When I was a younger player on the national team, I saw that Christie Pearce Rampone had her daughters with her at all of the camps. My sister was a nanny at one camp, and I saw how easy Christie made it look. Of course, the reality is it's not easy at all. It's really amazing what we moms are able to do in terms of resilience and figuring things out. Like if Charlie is on the road with me and I'm tired after training and want to maybe just stay in bed and relax, I know that's not an option. She wants to go out and explore the city, so that's what we do. But because I truly do love and prioritize my family over all else, I get it and I just make it work. It's not easy, but I feel more fulfilled now in being able to do everything that I want to do both professionally and in my personal life.

"When my husband, Servando, and I decided we wanted to have a baby, it was scary for sure. I didn't know if I could even have children. My mom is the only one of her siblings who could conceive. I had a lot of fear, but I had always imagined being a mom. Then when I got pregnant, it's like you're hit with so much at once. *How is this going to work when I give birth? Am I going to be supported enough? And what about when I come back as a professional athlete?* My doctor was saying, 'Oh you can exercise some, but don't raise your heart rate too much.' And I'm thinking to myself, *Well, have you ever worked with a professional athlete? Do you even know the sort of exercise that I do on a daily basis?*

"I did a lot of research on my own, but I felt like I didn't really know where to look for guidance. I reached out to a pelvic floor specialist, I reached out to a chiropractor, I did all of these things that I thought I should be doing, but I felt like it was really hard to be faced with all of these questions and wonder if I was doing it right. I know that every mom has dealt with that, but as a professional athlete, it felt like, *Okay, there should be more studies or better programs in place to help professional athletes as we go through pregnancy and post-pregnancy and return to play.* There's such a straightforward return-to-play procedure for a hamstring injury or an ACL injury but not so much for pregnancy. My hope is that teams or organizations like Team USA or the USOPC [U.S. Olympic and Paralympic Committee] create some sort of guide that can help serve as a support system for new moms. I think that's really important. [Authors' note: And others did, too. In August of 2024, FIFPRO, an organization for professional soccer players, launched a post-partum return to play guide. This comprehensive 48-page manual was developed by a task force that included several professional "soccer moms," one of whom was fellow Tough Mother Cheyna Matthews.]

"The three pillars of my Alex Morgan Foundation are sports equity, support for moms, and creating opportunities for girls. The mom thing didn't naturally fit into the foundation, but it was something that I was passionate about. A lot of times moms feel…not forgotten, but that they need to do everything, and that's just the way it is. Women are so good at multitasking in general. It's sickening! And sometimes it's to our detriment. Because we can do it all, we try to do it all. Women apparently are supposed to get more sleep than men, but how are we supposed to do everything with our job, with our child, and at home while also getting more sleep? The math there is just not mathin'.

"I feel like being a mother has changed me a ton. I'm more aware of female athletes and the responsibilities that we have and I have so much respect and admiration for working moms in general. I have chosen to be very visible about my life as a mom. I want to show my sponsors and the companies that I work with what this life can look like if we as working moms are supported. We've fought for the ability to bring our children on the road with us. We have support from our club teams, from U.S. Soccer, and I wanted to be able to take advantage of that. As much as I wanted to start a family, I also always wanted to continue to further my career. Being able to do both for me looked like Charlie traveling with me a lot and being my little mini-me as I went around the world playing.

"While focused on our playing careers, I think a lot of us moms in U.S. Soccer have tried to ask questions about why things are done the way that they are. With the Olympics in Tokyo, for example, when my daughter was one year old, I had a lot of questions, like 'Why aren't Olympians able to have their children at the Olympic village? And why isn't my childcare provider able to have credentials for certain things?' Why do the Olympics operate this way? Is that just because the average age of Olympians used to be 18 to 22, and now it's more like 22 to 30 and they just haven't kept up with the times? Has nobody questioned that?

"I want to push for better things not only for me, but also for the future of moms in sports. The Equal Pay settlement was a huge moment when it was signed in front of all of the fans and in front of my daughter, just knowing all of the years that we fought for this, that we did so much unpaid work, really, fighting this level of discrimination. My daughter most likely never will grow up in a world where she'll have to fight for that. I think that's really special, and having her share that moment with me was important. She may not have understood it at the time—she was two—but I'm proud that she'll be able to look back on that moment and know what we did.

I remember that moment as well. I was in the broadcast booth that day, and while watching the ceremony unfold live on the air, I was also watching Alex and Charlie and thinking, *What better reminder could there be of why these women are fighting for change?* Little Charlie, in her too big but still just right "Equal Pay" jersey, gazing lovingly up at her mother while Alex helped make history. Of course, Charlie also got restless and started tickling her mom's face with a scarf at one point, which definitely tickled me and almost made

me laugh out loud on air, but Alex remained focused on the task at hand. I
have loved following her journey both as a soccer player and as a mom, and
you rarely see her these days without her little "mini-me" by her side.

—J.H.

"There are these little moments that happen sometimes that make me feel really proud. The other night I was putting Charlie to bed, and she told me that she wants to play soccer like me when she grows up. It's not that I want her to play professional soccer when she grows up. I want her to be whatever she wants to be, but she sees what I'm doing and she also wants to be on that field making her family proud and doing something she thinks is amazing. She'll also say, 'I need to eat my vegetables and all my dinner, so I can be strong like Mommy.' The natural thing for a child to say might be 'Strong like Daddy,' but she sees both her Mommy and Daddy as strong. I think changing the way kids think in that little way is really special. That's part of the reason I love having her with me. There is minimal me time, and it's far from easy, but it's also really fun to be able to take her everywhere with me."

24
COURTNEY BANGHART

Main photo: AP Images

Courtney Banghart is the head women's basketball coach at the University of North Carolina. She joined the Tar Heels in 2019 after 12 years at Princeton, where in 2015 she was named the Naismith National Coach of the Year and one of Fortune's 50 Greatest Leaders. She has hitchhiked through Alaska, bungee jumped in Switzerland, was a finalist to appear on The Amazing Race, *and earned a degree in neuroscience from Dartmouth. So, it's no wonder that Banghart tackled motherhood with ferocious fearlessness. She and her wife, DJ, have twin boys, Eli and Tucker, born in 2014, and a daughter, Grey, born two years later. All three kids can often be spotted around the Tar Heels women's basketball team, but for that to happen, Banghart had to first convince herself that her children would not take away from her focus.*

"As a coach I am intense. I know that. It's part of who I am and how I operate. My players know what they're going to get from me, and I think part of my success as a coach has come from them knowing that I am all in all the time. Once I became a mother, that didn't change. Things might look a little different, and that's by design. My kids are constantly around me and my team, and I make no secret that I am both a coach and a mother. So many coaches over the years have reached out to me and said, 'Can you speak about this? Can you be a coach and have a family?' I mean, here I am doing it! But I get it. There are so many women out there wondering if this life is possible. I bet I have had no less than 25 meaningful conversations over the last five years with young coaches saying they feel like they'll probably have to leave the business to have a family.

I tell them, 'If you were in another career, like banking or law, and you wanted to be successful, you'd need to work just as many hours. You absolutely do not have to give up your career to be a mother.'

"I also try to tell the younger coaches—and this goes to all women thinking about becoming a mother—if you waited to take your SAT test until you were ready, you'd never have taken it. So, if you wait to have kids until you feel you have everything in place and it will be a smooth transition, you will never have kids. Do you want a life with children or do you want a life without? There is no in-between. It's that work/life synergy.

"Everyone's looking for that. Not really balance because I don't think you can find a perfect balance. When you're at work, you'll sometimes feel like you're not being a good enough parent. And when you're with your kids, you'll sometimes feel like you're not doing enough at work. For me, this internal struggle was the hardest part to get used to.

Ah, work/life synergy! I wish I had heard it phrased that way when my kids were younger. I struggled for so long trying to find balance. (I never even attempted to find the perfect one!) Those days stick with you: taking work calls when you're with the kids on the weekend or having to go on a last-minute business trip that nearly makes you miss your daughter's birthday party. (Sorry, Claire, you probably don't even remember that, but you can add it to the list!) So, for you working mamas, if you find yourself feeling frustrated because you can't strike a balance, maybe take a page from Coach's playbook and work toward synergy instead!

—A.L.

"My wife, DJ, carried all three of our children. So I didn't have the physical recovery that she did, but I felt it all mentally and emotionally. My head understood what I was trying to do, but my heart was constantly torn.

"Our twins were born in June, and for basketball July is a huge recruiting month. For a coach recruiting is the lifeblood of a program. So in July of 2014, when I was the head coach at Princeton, I was still recruiting. I'm sure some people judged me. My kids were only a month old. But I knew I needed to get out there. What was different was the way that I recruited. Rather than stacking two or three visits on top of each other, I would fly wherever I needed to go, then hop on a plane, and fly right back home before leaving again the next morning. Even if it was only for eight or 10 hours, it was worth it for me to fly home. For the first few weeks that the boys were born, I was splitting time. The twins were born premature, and they spent 26 days in the NICU [newborn intensive care unit]. DJ was pumping all that she could, going back and forth, and I was trying to run our summer basketball camp while also running back and forth to the hospital. I would go directly to work, then camp, then back to the hospital. This dizzying treadmill of responsibility, it becomes your new life. In a period of intense transition like that, it's only natural to question your investment in both places. Was I still as good professionally as I had been before? More importantly, was I a good mom?

"I had a lot of external validation that year. I went 30–0 in the regular season, was named the Naismith National Coach of the Year, and was recognized as one of 'The World's 50 Greatest Leaders' by *Forbes* (with the likes of Bill and Melinda Gates, Tim Cook, Taylor Swift, and the pope). And even with all of that, all of these people telling me that I was doing great, I was still doubting myself as a mother and a coach. I remember having a really impactful conversation with Craig Robinson. He had coached basketball at Brown and Oregon State while raising his kids, and his daughter, Leslie, was then playing for me at Princeton. So, when my wife was pregnant in 2014, I shared some of my concerns with Craig. I worried about the weight that I would put on DJ's shoulders, of all the time that she would have to care for the kids while I was at practice or games or on the road recruiting. I was sensitive to how my players might react, too; they were used to me being all in for them. Would becoming a mother make them feel that they were no longer my priority, my focus? What Craig said to me was so profound. Without hesitation he said, 'My hope is that you have those kids around all the time. As a parent I want my daughter to see a successful working mother. I want her to see that it's possible and that you can thrive in both areas. I want you to have your kids everywhere.'

"It was like a light came on for me, and damn if I didn't do it! When my Princeton team went 30–0 during that regular season, my boys were with me for the entire ride. Playing in the Ivy League, we had long bus trips, and those were brutal. But my twins and wife went to every single game home and away, traveling on the bus with us. The boys would be sitting behind the bench in their buckets, just like another bag of balls. With us all the time. My director of operations was great, always making sure that two cribs were requested for my hotel room well ahead of time on road trips. But our team took an early-season trip to Cancun in 2014, and when we arrived, there was only one crib available. The boys, about five months old at the time, were too little to sleep together—with me in the bed or with each other in the crib. Someone at the hotel suggested—and this is the God's honest truth—that we put pillows in the tub and let one of the babies sleep in there. *Um, no.* I'm exhausted from the trip, it's late, and so I start asking the hotel, 'Okay, what else do you have?' At one point, they say, 'How about a drawer?' *Well,* I thought to myself, *I guess it's better than a bathtub!* So we did it. I put one baby in the crib and one in a drawer that was on the floor next to my bed. You just figure it out. [Authors' note: It is somewhat incredible that not one—but two—of our Tough Mothers had to employ this baby-in-a-drawer technique! You may remember that U.S. Soccer player Christie Pearce Rampone did it, too.]

"That was also the year that we met the president. It was the first round of the 2015 NCAA Tournament, and president Barack Obama was in attendance. This was historic, as it marked the first time that a sitting president of the United States had attended an NCAA women's sporting event in person. President Obama's niece, Leslie Robinson, who I mentioned before, was a freshman on our Princeton team. The Obamas wound up sitting directly behind my family. However, I didn't even get to meet them. President Obama walked in a minute before the game—he probably couldn't get in earlier because of all the security—and that was when my players were running toward the bench. I had just told them in the locker room to stay locked in on me and I'd be locked in on them. So, President Obama meets the other coach and starts walking that 40 feet toward our bench. I could see it all happening out of the corner of my eye, but I just stayed locked in to my team. I never even looked up. The game starts, and that's that. My boys can say they met the president and gave him a high-five, but I did not!

"A lot of coaches have asked me if I feel like being a mother has hurt me in recruiting, if I've lost some of my edge. No way. As moms we are masters of efficiency. I don't watch movies. I don't have the time. So you do have to make some sacrifices. But I can still text and be in touch with my recruits when I'm up at night with the kids or I can hop in a car and bring them with me on a visit. Never are my children not going to be welcome in my workplace, and if at some point there is the perception that I'm less bought in, then this isn't the work for me. I still go back to what Craig and I talked about that day and I remind myself—and anyone else who asks—that we are mentors and leaders even as parents. It's not a weakness to be a parent, to let your players see you run them through skill workouts while you hold your baby in a sack on your chest. My accomplishments as a coach are rewarding, but it's my children who have brought color to my life. There is no replacement for the love and look of a child. There's just none."

PART VIII

HUMILITY

—JENN

Humility develops as you learn to have a good laugh at your own expense. This started out as a defense mechanism for me around middle school. I would laugh at myself—"Haha, I know, my chest is still so *flat*" or "Yes, you can see my Mickey Mouse socks sticking out from the bottom of my jeans because I am a dork and I am growing too fast." Apparently, no one else in junior high thought those socks were as cool as I did. So better to laugh with them than to be laughed at, right? Now, in the realm of motherhood, it's also a good reminder to laugh at yourself every now and then. And while motherhood presents many opportunities for humility—you put the diaper on backward, and now poop is all over the car seat; you forgot to add the pediatrician appointment to your calendar and now you have to wait another three months to get in; you can't seem to say one single thing to your teenage daughter without her stomping off in anger—for me nothing was quite so humbling as breastfeeding.

In fact, the exact moment that prompted me to write a book is still so fresh in my mind. Can I take you back in time for just a second? Picture it: I'm sitting there on my suitcase with my breasts in my hands, pumping my baby's milk, while stranger upon stranger walks past me. In the middle of a public restroom. In the busiest airport in the world.

I have interviewed Hall of Fame coaches, sat side by side with Olympic gold medalists and World Cup champions, and pointed a microphone in front of some of the most famous faces in sports. But with the lens of the women's restroom world focused upon me—or so I felt—I wanted no part of the spotlight. I wanted simply to be a mom, creating sustenance for her child without a thousand inquisitive eyes peering at my breasts, my pump, or my leave-me-alone-I-just-had-a-baby-a-few-months-ago-butt perched precariously on my suitcase. I had no affirmations. No high-fives from teammates telling me I could do it, no boob group (it's a thing) saying, "Yes, girl, me, too!" I felt desperate, anxious, and mortified. I looked nowhere but down. I prayed for the minutes to tick off my watch. I couldn't make eye contact with anyone or force a helpless smile to my face. I could only hold on and silently repeat the litany of curse words I had ready for whoever designed this Godforsaken mother-effing, not-nursing-friendly airport. I decided then and there that something good (besides the milk, of course) had to come of this. I would find a way to share my pain...and my pride.

That was basically the prologue for the first concept of this book. The title was *Milk on the Move*, and the idea was to focus specifically on the struggles of breastfeeding moms on the road. But Aimee and I made the conscious decision to move away from the focus on breastfeeding because we want this book to be for all mothers—whether you breastfeed or not. We support you and honor you in whatever choice you make in regards to feeding your baby. There is no right or wrong here—only what is best for you and your family. And we recognize that breastfeeding is just one of many humility-inducing aspects of motherhood.

That being said, it's probably no coincidence that there are a few more moments of milk-making mortification included in this tenet on humility. Arizona women's basketball coach Adia Barnes Coppa famously pumped while talking to her team at halftime of a national championship game. Reporter Katie Witham learned to squeeze in time to pump whenever, wherever, and in front of *whomever* she needed to get it done. I felt exposed in my aforementioned moment on the suitcase, but it is nothing to compared to what you'll hear from Katie and FOX Sports reporter Allison Williams.

There is something so liberating when you start talking about breastfeeding. We casually toss around terms like *nipple*, *boob*, or *areola*, and it kind of reminds me of a scene from *Old School* when Vince Vaughn's character tells his young son to cover his ears and put on "earmuffs," so the guys can say whatever curse words they want. Will Ferrell's character then begins reeling off whatever random bad words pop into his head. That's like us, right now. We can tell everyone else to put on their earmuffs and just start shouting about whatever breast-induced trauma we may be going through. The way your boobs look when they're being stretched in and out of the breast pump? Yeah, no one ever told me about that, which may be a good thing. But once you've seen your nipples stretched like Silly Putty and you eventually stop trying to cover up because it's just one more thing to worry about and your mother-in-law walks in while you're tired and topless, well, it all becomes a bit less taboo. We need to learn how to talk and laugh about these things because it will help us to *survive* these things.

With that in mind, I'm going to make myself real vulnerable and admit something that I am usually so embarrassed to talk about. But vulnerability is one of our tenets, right? And it kind of goes hand in hand with humility. I had a lot of trouble in the breastfeeding department, at least in part because I have fairly flat nipples. *Am I really writing this? Okay, deep breath.* I was always so self-conscious about my nipples growing up. They did not stick out the way that I saw other women's nipples do. Those headlights most women try to avoid while wearing tight shirts? I wished I could have had that problem. But while flat nipples were awkward during adolescence, that was nothing compared to what they meant for breastfeeding. It is not easy, as you might imagine, for a baby to latch on to a flat nipple. The nipples can be coaxed to come out some, but they will never stretch and extend the way a normal nipple does.

With my first daughter, Ashley, I tried and tried to get her to latch, constantly pumping after I fed her to make sure that she was getting enough milk. But, man, was it starting to hurt. My nipples were all ripped up. I finally stopped and called in lactation consultants when I noticed blood in the milk that I was pumping. I thought, *What am I doing? What should I be doing?* You'll only ask yourself these questions about one million times as a mother—in the first year. I couldn't imagine going through one more day of breastfeeding with the kind of pain that I was in and I was on Day Eight of the 365 that I had planned. We tried everything to help Ashley nurse, including something that finally provided me a little relief: the nipple shield. This lovely little silicone device looks kind of like (but not really) a real nipple and it fits over your own flattened or chewed-up nipple. I eventually found out a lot of people use these things. I thought I was the only one packing nipple protection, but Katie Witham did, too. And Allison Williams adamantly said to me, "Every new mom who wants to breastfeed should be told about nipple shields. I had no idea what they were or that they even existed until a nurse mentioned them to me, and all I can say is: 'game changer!'"

Using humor to help assuage our humiliation is definitely worthwhile, but we also acknowledge that there may come a time where laughter is not the best medicine. We don't want to make light of anyone's struggles and we know just how deep the pain can be if, for example, you want to breastfeed but can't. My friend Lindsey Lloyd, a producer at ESPN, opened up to me about her struggles in that department. Despite her best efforts—and she is a meticulous planner and researcher who tried everything to increase her milk production, from baking lactation cookies to guzzling more water and Pink Drinks at Starbucks—she just could not make enough milk for her baby. Desperate for any kind of help, she went to a breastfeeding class for new moms, hoping to find some solutions or at least be able to commiserate with some other women who were having the same challenges. Instead, Lindsey felt like she walked into a group of women who just needed an excuse to get out of the house. Rather than struggling to produce, they were joking about how much milk they were making. It was absolute torture for Lindsey.

On her drive home, more disheartened than ever, Lindsey's son, Owen, started bawling in the backseat. Worried, as she always was, that he was hungry from not getting enough milk, she pulled over to the side of the road, climbed into the backseat, and tried to feed him. It wasn't successful. This was one of the most traumatic moments of Lindsey's early life as a mother because, as she said, she felt like a total failure. She broke down in tears and cried there in the backseat along with her son. "In the moment, failure was all I could see. It took me that full experience to understand that breastfeeding is really not meant to be for every mother. I beat myself up pretty good about it. I'm not a very open person when it comes to my personal experiences, but I want other moms to understand that they, too, may feel some of the same challenges with this natural process that was anything but natural to my body. And if you do, give yourself some grace," she said. "I hope...moms who may be struggling will really hear those words and will give yourself a break."

Such great advice. And fear not, my non-breastfeeding mamas, this section and the amazing women within it have plenty more to offer beyond their breastfeeding experiences. Allison Williams' message about "mothering out loud" is one of the best, most empowering mantras that you'll ever find. And Katie Witham's Lionel Messi-induced mom guilt is something we can all relate to—even if we don't get up close and personal with one of the greatest soccer players of all time. For Adia Barnes Coppa, her determination to "have it all" reflects the desire and the challenges that working moms know all too well.

25

ADIA BARNES COPPA

Adia Barnes Coppa was a bad ass from the start. She set records as a high school player, was named Pac-10 Player of the Year, and led the University of Arizona Wildcats to their first ever NCAA appearance. She then went on to become the first women's player at Arizona to be drafted into the professional leagues. After playing in the WNBA and overseas, Barnes Coppa moved into coaching, returning to her alma mater as the head women's basketball coach in 2016. Her husband, Salvo, is one of her assistant coaches, and the pair share their basketball life with their son, Matteo, and daughter, Capri. What Barnes Coppa didn't necessarily expect was to share intimate details of her working mom life with a national television audience on ESPN, but that's exactly what happened during the 2021 NCAA women's championship game. ESPN's Holly Rowe reported that Barnes Coppa was late coming out at halftime because she was still in the locker room pumping. Rowe, a working mom herself, proudly added, "For those of you who think this is too much information, I'm just going to tell you this: let's normalize working mothers and all that they have to do to make it all happen."

"I never planned to do that and I certainly didn't plan for the whole world to hear about it when Holly gave her report, but now I'm glad she did. If it wasn't the national championship game, I would never have pumped at halftime. I would have had time before the game. But when I got there, I had media obligations. I couldn't get there as early as I wanted and I was so stressed. I figured I wouldn't make as much milk, but in the game, I started getting that tight feeling like I needed to pump. My boobs felt like they were at my chin. I was petrified of leaking, too. I didn't want milk on my shirt in the national championship game. So, I was like, I gotta go pump.

"Now, I'm not popping out my boob in front of everybody, but I'm not shy about breastfeeding. I can't be. So it's halftime of the national championship game and it's a tight game. Our team got off to kind of a slow start, but we picked it up in the second quarter, and we trailed Stanford by seven points at the half [before eventually losing by one]. I had my pump on and I went to the locker room to talk to the team. I had put a cover over it, but they obviously knew I was pumping. As I'm talking the cover drops, and my face gets all red. I pick it up, cover up again, pause, and the players all just start cracking up. You could see my hands-free bra, my nipples through the pumps, and everybody's eyes got big. Then they just started laughing. I'm thinking, *Well, at least I broke the ice*. It lightened up a stressful moment at my expense, but that's okay!

As the daughter of a cartoonist, I always appreciate a little humor and humility to break the ice, but even more I appreciate Adia's honesty. For those of us who nursed our babies, which I did for three months with both of my kids, we each have a story. I never pumped. A friend, who was a few years older than I, tried to sell me on it, but once she described the clunky contraption that she had rented from the medical supply store, I quickly decided we would supplement with formula. On those evenings when I got home late and missed my nighttime nursing routine, well, let's just say it ain't pretty when supply far exceeds demand!

—A.L.

"I never would have told Holly I was pumping. I probably would have said what every mother does: 'Oh, I had to go to the bathroom' or something like that. There are so many games I'm putting a bra pad in, fixing my straps, then I step on the court all calm. That's pretty much every game. But this time I was coming out so late, and when Holly asked what was going on, someone on my staff just said, 'She's pumping.'

"After the game I started hearing from so many people, not only about the game, but also about Holly's report. I was shocked it was such a thing. But also happy. If I can help create a voice for women, that's pretty awesome. And it was organic. I wasn't showing this other side of me intentionally. I didn't realize all these women felt the same way. I just thought, *This is my situation*. So it was like, *Wow, you've gone through this, too?* They would say their breastfeeding or pumping experiences were stressful and embarrassing and they didn't feel like they could talk about it. That's sad! We shouldn't have to hide anything about being mothers. We should be proud. And we need to support one another. How do we not? Support women! We shouldn't always be an afterthought. There should be a place for women to breastfeed in every arena, in every place that women go to work. There should be changing tables in men's and women's restrooms. There should be more family restrooms. If women designed more of these buildings, they would be designed differently, I promise you.

"Every woman in this business has a concern if they're thinking about starting a family. We push back having kids or don't have as many kids because we're scared. We don't have a lot of time. It's a choice that I made—to have a family—because I wasn't going to let my profession dictate my family life. I was going to find a way to make it all work. Do I feel guilty sometimes? Yes. Do I miss things sometimes? Yes. But I can do both—even if it means baring my boobs and pumping in front of my team at halftime of the biggest game of my life or being up all night before the semifinal game and having my baby, Capri, spit up and poop on me before it was even 5:00 AM! I had to share that. So I put it on Instagram, and it kind of went viral. But I wanted to put it out there because unless you're a mom, you just don't get it. This is what we do. This is what we deal with. It's not easy, but we do it.

"I won't lie. I did have a few breakdowns during that NCAA Tournament. We were in a bubble because it was 2021 and we were dealing with the pandemic. So there I am in a bubble with a six-year-old and a six-month-old. You can imagine. Sometimes my son, Matteo, would be running around like crazy, and I was just like, *I just need a second to cry.* Then I'd have to pick myself up, say, *You got this. You're good.* And keep going. It's still hard. My husband, Salvo, is on my staff. So we're both busy. We don't have a lot of family around to help, but I'm not gonna *not* do my job. I'm not gonna quit. We're going to find a way to make it work."

Katie Witham has been a host and sideline reporter for FOX, ESPN, the Big Ten Network, the Cleveland Guardians, Charlotte FC, and the Columbus Crew. In 2023 Witham joined Apple TV as a reporter to help cover Inter Miami and global superstar Lionel Messi. She and her husband, Richie, had their first son, Owen in 2019 and their second son, Cole in 2021. Witham's ability to do her job while also being so humble and quick to laugh at herself is one of the things that makes her such a great teammate, as you'll hear from her former FOX Sports broadcast partner, John Strong. No doubt Witham's boys, when they are old enough to know as much, will tell you that it's part of what makes her such a wonderful mom, too. Not that they'll necessarily be privy to some of the stories you're about to hear. These are meant for the ears of working moms only!

"**B**eing a woman working in sports, sometimes you are the only woman that has a seat at the table, and I felt that I needed to prove why I deserved that seat. I put off becoming a mother because I had that seat. And then after I had my first son, Owen, I went back to work when he was four-and-a-half weeks old. I was breastfeeding, pumping, traveling, working, trying to manage all of the things that you do as a working mom. And I think I felt even more of a need to prove that I could do it and do it well and be a mom, which led, I think, to some pretty crazy moments.

"I was determined to breastfeed, but the struggles with breastfeeding? I feel like I had them all. They say it's the most natural thing, and it is once you get the hang of it. That took me a while and a few lactation consultants and a nipple shield and a hickey on my left breast. And mastitis. Breastfeeding Owen was the hardest thing that I've ever done. And pumping on the road? Let me tell you: it just plain sucks. I was covering Major League Soccer when Owen was born. My first game back, I went like six-and-a-half hours and was way overdue to pump. I looked like Dolly Parton! The zipper on my jacket was pulling, and I was definitely panicking. This particular stadium, I couldn't even find a bathroom. It just had Porta Potties everywhere, and I was like, *I cannot! My baby is four-and-a-half weeks old. I cannot pump his milk in a PortaPotty.* I wound up going to this semi-truck that was parked next to our TV production truck. I'm not entirely sure what its purpose was, but at that point, I didn't care. I was desperate. There was one guy working in there, and oh my God, it was so awkward. He let me in and then started trying to clean up. There were pop cans lying around, bags of Cheetos. This poor guy practically lives in this truck, and here I am asking to come in and put on a breast pump. I think he was more embarrassed than I was at that point, and I was pretty mortified.

"I'll tell you what, though, my Willow pump was an absolute lifesaver. It's fantastic. It's concealed. You can put it in your bra, and it just basically looks like two boobs that you put on top of your boobs. It allows you to pump discreetly around people—at least most of the time. Our crew was doing interviews the day before a match, and I thought we had a little break. So I ran into the bathroom and put my Willow pump on. I tried to cover up my larger-than-life chest—this pump does make you look pretty well-endowed—and returned to our interview room. Sitting there along with our crew is DC United head coach Ben Olsen. I decided there was no holding back. So I said, 'Hi, I have a pump on and I'll be doing it during this interview. Sorry, not sorry, I need to feed my kid. You may hear a slight noise every now and then. That's the milk.' Ben is frozen. He looks at me, looks at [my broadcast partners] John and Stu, looks back at me, and says, 'You're seriously wearing a pump right now?' He was intrigued and started asking questions about my portable pump—referencing that his wife had breastfed all of their kids and commenting on all the wires she had running everywhere and how loud her pump was. He made us all laugh, made it completely normal, and was totally fine that I was pumping in front of all of them.

"I think becoming a mother has actually made me more confident. It has helped me find my voice more and made me more efficient because I have to be. I've learned more about what I need and what I want out of life. I've gotten a taste of everything: of full-on working, then having a child, and continuing to work and travel, to then just staying home full time with both boys during the pandemic. Then during my stay-at-home-mom stretch, MLS calls and says, 'Messi's coming, and we're going to have one reporter for the English broadcasts and we want it to be you.' My husband, Richie, and I met playing college soccer and he was like, 'You've got to do it. We'll make it work.'

"It was kind of like being part of a traveling circus…in the best way! But it was wild. Originally, it was supposed to be three games. Then it turned into like 18 games in less than three months. We couldn't catch our breath at home. It was a whirlwind! [Authors' note: Right at this moment, an upside-down nose slides in front of Katie's camera. She laughingly shoos her oldest son away and helps him find some sort of counting program on television.] Screen time—that's how we survived Messi! No, not really, but we just had to figure it out on the fly. My husband bent over backward for me to be able to travel and cover Messi. They say it takes a village when you have a kid, right? And how true that is. My mom came in, my sister would help out, Richie was all hands on deck and was still working his job. I'm so grateful for such a strong support system. But I don't think I ever had a drive to the airport without tears. I live about 13 minutes from the airport and I would cry for about 12 of them. I mean, mom guilt is real! And does it ever truly go away? Because it hasn't yet!

The comforting, been-there-gone-through-that mama in me wants to reassure Katie and all of you that *yes, it does go away!* But platitudes are not what we promised you. Here's the deal—Mom Guilt is real and it rarely ever goes away completely. Even the world-renowned Cleveland Clinic agrees that Mom Guilt is a thing. But like everything else in your working mom life, *you can handle it.* Is it going to eat you up at times? Yes. Will it factor into many of the decisions that you make? Probably. And that's okay. Acknowledge that it's there and remind yourself that it's called Mom Guilt—not Kid Guilt—for a reason. These situations that split you down the seams are almost always harder on you than they are on your kids. The guilt will ebb and flow as your children (and you) grow, and you will learn when to listen to it and when to shove it aside and soldier on.

—*J.H.*

"I'm type A. I like to be in control and do things my way. Then you become a mother and you realize you control nothing in life. I am humbled by these tiny humans every single day. And I'm humbled by motherhood. You always have this idea of how it's going to go…and then you become a parent and you're like, 'Whoa!' We're all baptized by fire when we have a child and become a parent.

"I'm the middle child of three and growing up I was never the smartest. I was just like the ornery, loud kid that had to work really hard for everything in life. My television career? I was the same way. You know how many times I was told, 'You didn't play professional soccer. Who are you to come in here?' But I've always had to work my—excuse my language—ass off for everything. Being a mom and being a working mom, I've continued to have to work my tail off. All moms are tough because you have to be. I'm one definition of a tough mom. Everyone's motherhood journey is completely different. There are things that you know innately as a mom. Even if you have no idea what you're doing—because no one does. We're all still trying to figure it out every single day. Relying on your intuition is huge. There's something to be said for being a working mom in any capacity. You are showing your kids that you can juggle different things. I am trying to raise two men that are kind and respectful and empathetic and inclusive and support women, especially women who want to work and do different things. And so for them, seeing Mommy go out and work, I'm proud to set that example for them no matter how many tears I have to shed.

When Katie first started talking about getting pregnant, she'd say, "Sorry if this is weirding you out." I'm married, I have two kids, and so I said, "There's really nothing that you can do or say that will throw me off or gross me out." I've seen it all, done it all. With my son, Jake, I was in charge of the breast pump and had to clean and organize all of the parts and store and catalogue all of the milk. And so I wanted to be as supportive as I could for Katie. As a broadcast team, we all took a big role in each others' lives. We were like each others' road family because we spent so much time together. We talked a lot. We were like, "Tell us when you're ready." If anything, we didn't want her to rush back.

My broadcast partner, Stu Holden, is a dad, too. Having kids, going back to work, it's easy for us guys. It's so different for her as a mom. We didn't take that lightly. We were making sure rehearsals and pregame work flow were optimized so that she was pumping at the right time. I would ask if she wanted me to get an ice pack to buy her a few extra minutes, trying to help and support her that way. All new moms need that. It's really difficult when you go back to work. Katie always hated when we'd make a big deal of it; she didn't want it to seem like she was this big hero. We said, "No, you deserve a lot of credit for what you're having to do." Her on-air performance was never affected. Her ability to juggle it all is a testament to what a good pro she is and what a good mom she is as well.

Our running joke was how long we'd be into the weekend before she started talking about pumping. She'd say, "I'm not going to talk about my breasts at all this weekend." Then we'd go, "Yeah, sure, Katie." We teased her endlessly. After games we'd pile into the rental car, and she'd say, "All right, boys, eyes front. I've got to do something back here!" Then you'd hear these slurping sounds from the pump, and she'd be shaking stuff out the window. We were just like, "Don't get breast milk on the rental car!" It's hard enough to be a mom, but to be a woman in broadcasting and have to combine those two things is a lot. She—like all working moms—deserves all the credit.

—John Strong, FOX Sports play-by-play announcer
and Witham's former broadcast partner

27
ALLISON WILLIAMS

You know that old cliche about one door closing and another one opening? Well, Allison Williams is living proof that when you're ready to walk through that new door you just might find something on the other side that is unexpectedly, breathtakingly perfect. In 2019 Williams was a new mom working her butt off at ESPN. Just about every week, she was flying across the country from her home in California—with her baby, Lyle, often in tow—reporting from the sidelines for college football or basketball or working in studio as a host. Then the COVID-19 pandemic hit. In the fall of 2021 for the first time in 15 years, Williams was absent from the sidelines of college football. She explained why she was stepping away in a post on Twitter: "While my work is incredibly important to me, the most important role I have is as a mother. Throughout our family planning with our doctor, as well as a fertility specialist, I have decided not to receive the COVID-19 vaccine at this time while my husband and I try for a second child." The following year Williams gave birth to her daughter, Lexi, and signed a contract with FOX Sports. Her workload was less than what she had been doing in the past, which turned out to be the best thing that could have happened for Williams and her family.

"I am so incredibly thankful for the role and the workload that I have now. It's just enough for me to feel fulfilled professionally and also feel like I'm not missing out at home. The whole experience of going through COVID, not working, and then having my second child, it just made me realize how important my role as a mom was, and I don't know if I valued it enough. I knew it was the most important role, but I don't think I realized how irreplaceable I was in my own home. I garnered a lot of my intrinsic value from working outside the home, and that whole experience was a wake-up call for me, that it's actually the other way around. I am very much replaceable by my employer; I am not replaceable with my family. So I learned to value and prioritize and really celebrate and cherish my role as a mom.

"I want women to 'mother out loud.' I don't want them to mother quietly. I don't want them to mother and be embarrassed or feel like they have to hide it. Mom out loud. Talk about breastfeeding. Talk about pumping. Talk about being exhausted or starving or whatever it is because the more we can normalize the challenges of motherhood—and also celebrate the amazing rewarding parts—the more women will realize that it can be done and that it's worth it. That was something that was different for me from my first child to my second. With my first I felt like I had to present like nothing was going to change. It's no big deal. 'I'm still Allison Williams, sideline reporter, I'm still a professional. I'm still 100 percent who I was.' Well, guess what? I actually wasn't, and that's okay. And so with my second child, Lexi, I didn't try to hide it. I didn't try to act like it wasn't hard. I am dealing with something that no one else on my crew is dealing with: a human life is dependent on me. That's exceptional! It's a blessing, and I'm so thankful for that. But my experience during the week, on a weekend, and traveling…is not theirs. They are certainly not thinking about places to pump or how to get a baby to latch or how to transport breastmilk, and that was a weekly occurrence for me.

"I've told other moms the only easy thing about breastfeeding is the decision to do it. What's so crazy to me is that while breastfeeding is natural and innate there are so many things that have to happen to make it successful. The latch is like this magical, mysterious, elusive thing when you first start. And, damn, does it hurt! I would wither in pain, toes curled, wanting to scream when Lyle would latch, but at the same time, I was so elated because he was on! And, man, as much as I loved breastfeeding—and I did really come to love it—I hated pumping. I pumped every day multiple times a day to build a stash. I made lactation cookies, took natural supplements, and drank a ton of water to boost my supply. When I had to travel without Lyle, I would take the last red-eye out and first flight back to minimize my time away from him. It was 48 hours, and that was the absolute max that I could swing being away with my supply of milk. I wrote out a schedule for my husband and left instructions on each milk packet as to when to feed Lyle. And I drove it home to him on repeat of just how important it was to not waste a drop. I was a total freak about my milk! I know that I hit a wall around four months. I just felt like I couldn't keep up. When I would have to pump for days at a time, I would just tell myself how lucky I was to have the ability to produce this milk. And pumping was helping me to continue to do a job that I loved and still be the mom that I wanted to be. I tried to be grateful instead of hateful toward my pump, ha!

"I returned to work when Lyle was eight weeks old. He traveled with me to games for the first several weeks of that football season, and that was great, but we did have some adventures. One Saturday I was in Louisville, Kentucky, for a matchup between the Louisville Cardinals and the Clemson Tigers. My husband, Sam, was at the game with Lyle, and we had planned for them to come meet me at halftime. The plan was for me to do my interview with one of the coaches, then sprint to my designated spot to nurse and pump. Let me pause for a second and say that my operations staff was just amazing. They made my breastfeeding needs a priority, and that was the greatest blessing ever. I never worried about having a place to pump pregame or at the half of football games. I knew it was taken care of. On this particular occasion, the ops team had found me a room to use that was not too far from the field. There was a caveat, however. The room was one that the EMTs [emergency medical technicians] might need to use if there was an injury or medical situation. I figured we'd be fine. Boy, was I wrong.

"When I went running off the field at halftime, I found the room was occupied. Time was ticking. I was getting desperate, and that's when one of the EMTs suggested that I use…the ambulance. It stays parked in the tunnel for emergencies, and it was free. So I was like, 'Okay, let's go!' With so little time, I knew I needed both the pump and my baby; there was no time to let him nurse both sides. I got into the ambulance, hiked down the top of my dress, hooked up one boob to the pump, and put Lyle on the other. Half-dressed but fully expressed!

"I tell you what, though, and all new moms out there, I hope you hear me on this: I think being around other women who were confident and unapologetic about breastfeeding gave me the security and courage to breastfeed or pump in public. That's what I mean about mothering out loud. We all know how uncomfortably close we have to sit next to strangers on airplanes. Feeding your newborn next to a man you've never met isn't exactly awesome. But I just kind of said, 'Fuck it.' I have to do what is best for my baby, and that is breastfeeding him right here, right now.

"And honestly, I was surprised at how kind, understanding, and just awesome people were. Men often shared what their wives went through, how old their kids were, things like that. Women talked glowingly about their new grandbabies and how they missed them. It was a great reminder that, no matter our differences, we were all babies in our mothers' arms at some point.

"And now with social media we actually have a platform that allows us to show what we're going through. We can show that we are moms, so people can see the personal stuff and they can see that we have this other role and this other life. And we can show how we do it. I think about people like Sam Ponder, who was a new mom when she was traveling around on *College Game Day*, and seeing that be a positive experience for her absolutely influenced me in knowing that it would be okay when I had to travel as a mom.

> Wow, a vote for social media as a *good* thing! My husband likes to say that social media will be "the death of society," and I have to say, I'm often inclined to agree with him, but Allison makes a good point. There is strength and empowerment in seeing other working moms succeeding...as long as you don't beat yourself up by comparison. That's why I always appreciate those people who reveal their flaws and failures along with their moments of triumph.
>
> —J.H.

"I've often wanted to make a reel of the *real* shit! I should be recording the meltdowns and the blowouts on the airplane, but when you're dealing with the chaos, it's a little hard to record it. I try to share moments that help people realize that I am a person, too. And when I'm not on TV or I'm not around, this is why. This is how my world is filled and occupied. But you have to keep it real. I never want to set unrealistic expectations for people because it's not all perfect and pretty and Instagram friendly. It's messy and it's ugly, and there are three of us at home while my husband is at work—me and the kids. I always tell people if two out of the three are showered or bathed and dressed at some point, that is a successful day. Three for three is knock it out of the park. We must be going somewhere. "There's quiet, unappreciated work that goes into any athlete achieving a goal, and there is so much quiet, unappreciated, unseen work that goes into being a good mom. Athletes will tell you that the game is not won in those 60 minutes or four quarters of a game; it's won in the two-a-day practices and the 5:00 AM workouts and the extra lifts. It's won when nobody's looking. I think it's the same with being a good mom. There is so much work that nobody sees or acknowledges, but that's what makes for the happiest of childhoods. We as moms are the magic makers. A lot of times what goes into making that magic, nobody sees. But the end result of having a child that is healthy and happy and thriving, who looks back on their childhood with joy and love—that's winning the greatest game in life."

PART IX
SUPPORT

—AIMEE

Support can come in many different forms—parents, a partner, friends, co-workers, teammates, children. If you're really lucky, it can come from a company culture created from the top down, like at Angel City FC, where every employee is encouraged to bring their whole self to the workplace. Some of us, like Florida State women's basketball coach Brooke Wyckoff, are used to showing up for others, but when we let those people support *us* when we need it, well... that can allow for something truly magical to happen. And sometimes you find the support you need in the most unexpected places, like I did with my boss' wife, actress Susan Saint James Ebersol. By sharing some of her own working mom experiences, she made me feel less alone...and in doing so inspired me to pay it forward and help those who followed in our working mom footsteps. And support can even come from forward-thinking entrepreneurs who fill a need or two, like Mamava's Sascha Mayer and Milk Stork's Kate Torgersen.

Wherever it comes from, whatever it looks like, let's agree that we can't do this thing without the support of others. From the very start, my parents encouraged me to reach for the stars. I didn't quite know what that meant back then, but I knew they believed in me. And that belief never wavered. I had great friends to lean on through the drama of adolescence and beyond. And I'm lucky to have a husband who's been by my side through the mess of it all.

But I never needed support as much as I did when I became a working mom. Whether it was taking a weekly walk and whine (or sometimes wine!) with my friend to talk about the real shit we were dealing with, the women who helped with my kids when I was away on various business trips, or my sister, who chose a different path as a stay-at-home mom but supported me through every step of mine, as they say, it took a village.

But in the office, it didn't take me long to notice that there weren't really any female role models (mommy mentors) to whom I felt connected. Although I wish I could have had them, I focused on trying to be that person for others. There's something so powerful about building a sisterhood, a community willing to talk openly about the good, the bad, and even the ugly, which is exactly what we set out to create for you here! Many of our Tough Mothers talk about how important their ride-or-die friends are. Having these allies isn't just about making us feel better, either; it's pretty essential to our survival as working moms. I came across an episode of *Your Mom* podcast in which they talked about the many ways a sisterhood is good for our mental health.

It's no surprise that connecting with other people is a basic human desire. After all, humans are social pack animals, and we need to be a part of a culture that helps each other. And that goes beyond the sisterhood, right? I had support from many of my male bosses and colleagues pretty early on. I don't think they realized how important it was to me, but when they asked me questions about my family and encouraged me to talk openly about my kids at work, that helped me as I tried to find some sense of balance...or synergy...in my life.

I'll let you in on a little Leone family secret: I never read fairy tales to my kids. When I read them as a child, I always wanted to know what happened at the end, but all I was told was that "they lived happily ever after." I mean, isn't that where the next chapter was supposed to begin? Or was I just a skeptic and a realist from a very young age? I never expected a knight in shining armor and I certainly didn't believe that a beautiful girl in eternal sleep could be awakened by the kiss of a handsome prince. For me Aesop's Fables had the more practical ending I was looking for. (Cue the eye roll from my kids.) These stories have morals like: "United we stand; divided we fall," "No one believes a liar even when he tells the truth," and, of course, the very valuable "once a wolf, always a wolf." To this day my kids accuse me of having a moral to just about every story in our lives.

The moral of this story is that everyone needs a little help and support sometimes. As Tough Mothers we don't always know how to ask for it, but most of us will appreciate it. Or as Aesop himself said in The Horse and the Donkey, "We should always be friendly to others and help those in need." See how I did that, kids?

28

ANGEL CITY FC

Alex Mallen

Lisa Milner Goldberg

Joscelyn Shumate Bourne

Angela Hucles Mangano

Julie Uhrman

Angel City FC prides itself on being a club that broke the mold for women's professional soccer. The Los Angeles-based franchise did it by investing in the community and demolishing pre-existing notions of what a women's professional team could be. The ownership group includes Hollywood stars like Natalie Portman, Eva Longoria, and Jennifer Garner; U.S. soccer legends like Mia Hamm, Abby Wambach, and Julie Foudy; and some of the biggest names in women's sports like Serena Williams, Billie Jean King, and Candace Parker. In 2024 Bob Iger and Willow Bay became the new majority owners of the club, making it the most valuable women's sports team in the world.

From the start, working moms have been a part of the very foundation on which Angel City is built. There are those you see, like striker Sydney Leroux, a mom of two who has always been very open and often hilariously honest about her experiences as a mother, and defender Sarah Gorden, mom to son Caiden, who told us that she hates the idea of people looking at her like some sort of a superhero. "We're just humans. We get it wrong all the time," she said. "We have guilt. I'm just a mom and an athlete trying to figure it all out." But there are also moms making it work behind the scenes at Angel City, and you'll hear from five of them. You'll see what a culture of support for working moms really looks like and how amidst the #acfc-mom-juggle-struggle—that's the clever name of the Slack channel that many of the moms use—it infuses strength and confidence throughout the entire company. We start at the top with Angel City president and co-founder Julie Uhrman.

"**A** lot of times you're accepted as the role you have. *I'm a coach, I'm a player.* But we want to look at the whole person. Maybe that means you're married, you're divorced, you have kids. *How do we support the whole person from an organizational standpoint?* We're intentional about it. We want to create an environment that we as females want to be a part of. In one of the first conversations that I had with Natalie Portman, we were talking about stadiums, and she said, 'What about the bathrooms? Do we have a special area for moms if they bring young kids?'

"We've always looked at it from a holistic standpoint but also very much through a female lens, especially knowing that in sports women have always been a minority and an afterthought. The product, the entertainment, the experience, that has never been tailored toward women. We were really intentional about building an experience that is tailored for all. Whether it's pay, maternal/ paternal leave, opportunities for development and promotion, opportunities for growth, if you take an equitable lens, everybody wins. If we create the best environment for working moms, it tells you as an employee or a player that it's okay to take time off and have a kid. You know that when you come back you'll have a club that has an environment that is incredibly welcoming and supportive of you as a mother because it's hard.

"We as women give everything to our work, we give everything to our kids, we give everything to our family, to our friends. If anybody in women's football or women's sports wants to talk about Angel City and what we're doing, what we're building, I make the time. I don't say no to anything because I want to grow the sport, I want to drive toward equity, I want to drive attention. So the concept of balance gets even harder because I am constantly putting myself out there and not asking for anything in return. I do it because I really do want to make the world a better place, and that gets prioritized, too.

So I always replace the word *balance* with *presence* because balance isn't real. Balance means that you're giving an ample amount of time to work, an ample amount of time to your kids, and you are present when you're doing both of those things and are singularly focused on that activity. And then if we're truly talking about balance, it's also self-care, self-development, socialization with friends. It's in all aspects of your life. For me, being a working mom is really more of an exercise in prioritization than balance. When is work going to be most important? When are my kids most important? How can I fit them both in?

"As mothers we're always juggling. If you can juggle, you can be a mom and a businesswoman. Any thought that you can't be great at both is a myth. You can absolutely be great at both. It's about prioritization, dedication, commitment, passion, presence. Finding a way to create a sense of harmony between work, life, and kids versus balance. If you're intentional with your actions, you can be great at both."

—Julie Uhrman, Angel City FC president
and co-founder, mom to Elle and Charlie

* * *

"It's nice to be able to be my whole self. I'm very professionally driven as are the other working moms that I've been fortunate to work alongside, but it's nice to come in and be able to say, 'I was researching this injury and how to manage it when I was interrupted by my toddler who had a three-part story for me' or 'my six-year-old decided he has some thoughts on my parenting style and what changes we should make. Have you dealt with this?'

"I'm fortunate to work at a place where my kids have the opportunity to be around a lot of strong, amazing women who show them how they beat the odds and have created a community of support for each other and embraced my family as well. At the end of my first season working with ACFC, we were on a Zoom call and—as often happens for me—I had a kid or two that decided they wanted to participate. Julie Uhrman paused the meeting and said, 'Joscelyn, how come I had no idea you had not one but *two* kids? I need to know more about this!' And she actually followed up on it. At previous jobs I found myself shying away from disclosing information about my family, and here is Julie, this amazing businesswoman, asking me to show *all* of me, my family included. It's such a great feeling."

—Joscelyn Shumate Bourne, Angel City FC director of rehabilitation and return to play, mom to Jayce and Jerome

* * *

"The support that I received from my colleagues throughout my entire pregnancy and since our little one was born has been incredible. I truly feel that I can be open and honest with our team and feel there is so much understanding and willingness to share advice and support. Whenever I see a successful woman working in sports who is also a mom, I am inspired to see it's possible. I think it's these examples that made me feel more at ease about having a baby at 40 as someone who has always been very career-driven. While it's a different experience for everyone and it's just extremely hard no matter who you are, just seeing women be both and talk about the challenges makes it feel real and less scary about the unknown."

—Alex Mallen, Angel City FC senior director of corporate partnerships, mom to Max

* * *

"Being around other working moms has made me feel like I'm not alone in navigating the trials of working motherhood. I don't feel like people have always talked about how hard it is, and by having co-workers that are also moms, we can commiserate on what is tough and also celebrate what is great in a way that other co-workers don't fully understand and wouldn't be expected to. There is a saying about how working moms 'are supposed to work like you don't have kids and parent like you don't work,' which I don't feel is the case at Angel City. If I have to take my daughter to the doctor and miss a meeting, no one has ever made me feel badly about it. They always cover for me. My male colleagues, too, some who don't have kids, also feel a license to step up and help in a way that I haven't experienced elsewhere. No one bats an eye when there is a kid in the background of a Zoom call or when we bring our kids to an event or to the office. It is part of the culture and a part I truly appreciate. Moms are such doers. We have to be efficient and be able to multitask. I can do like four different things while listening to a call and fully hear it because I have to do that all the time at home."

—Lisa Milner Goldberg, Angel City FC vice president of public relations, mom to Zoe and Ruby

* * *

"The biggest connection that I've experienced between sports and motherhood is the power of being a part of a team and the it-takes-a-village statement. At work there is a comfort in knowing that a lot of my colleagues have an understanding and empathy for each other as moms working in the same environment. At home my wife and I have different roles in our family team, and our children have their own unique personalities. How I've learned and am still learning to navigate the different stages of childhood and stay connected with my children is very reminiscent of my playing days in sports and being a part of a team. Being intentional, having a road map, a family vision, and figuring out what the special skills and abilities are that we each have to uplift one another, those are all lessons that I've seen and learned in sporting environments, too.

"We try not to balance but to blend work and family as often as we can, bringing the kids to games, having them around my Angel City colleagues. My son loves all sorts of animals and creatures and has now created a game that I bring in some of his toy insects and reptiles to our training facility to scare the coaches. I've filmed putting the toys in different chairs, laptops, lunch plates, and then seeing the reactions of the staff. He still hasn't realized that they are acting through all of it, but it brings him a lot of joy. We all crack up as a staff seeing who can bring the Best Actor Award nominee in, and I feel connected to my family while I'm still at work.

"It's a life-altering experience becoming a mother. There's this duality that occurs. Your experience with your child is special and your own, but you are also aware that yours are the experiences millions of others have also gone through. There's a lot of comfort that goes into knowing that. I have felt that with my own mother, too. I think about her, her caring and appreciation, how seriously she took parenting and motherhood, and just how much she did for us as children. There were times when I was younger that she was literally doing everything—working, raising us kids, cooking, cleaning—every aspect of house and home and family while also developing her own career. When my brother was born, I was four years old. So my mom had a four-year-old, a newborn, and she was completing her PhD! My mom has always been a superhero to me. Her devotion to being a good parent—I felt it then, of course, but

I really appreciate it as a mother now myself. And I definitely have her voice in my head. I mean, she is a psychologist. So sometimes, especially in my teenage years, I maybe wished I had a little less of her voice in my head. But now it's like this built-in support system. She definitely was such a strong figure for me in my life and still is to this day.

"You step into this other place and you see your parents differently once you are in that same role. For me and my mother, and I think for all women who become mothers, it's like a sisterhood. The stories you can tell, the shared experiences. When I had my son, Huntley, I really leaned on that sisterhood. My wife, Meg, carried our second child, Avyanna, and I'm so glad that we have both been able to go through that physical and emotional experience. And motherhood, as my mother often reminds me, is a lifelong commitment. Your responsibilities may look a little different at each stage, but you never stop being a mother. One time when Huntley was a toddler, we decided to make cupcakes for Meg for her birthday. We were putting the candles on, and he leans over—Huntley had this long, wild, curly hair—and his hair catches on fire! I quickly patted him down and put it out, but when I was telling my parents the story later, I was still feeling all of that anxiety. It was like I had PTSD; I saw flames and burning and had all of these terrible thoughts of disaster flying through my mind. That's when my mother said, 'Well, honey, it's a lifetime thing. Unexpected things are always going to happen. This is what it means to be a parent.'"

—Angela Hucles Mangano, Angel City FC general manager 2002–24, current Houston Dash general manager, two-time Olympic gold medalist in soccer, mom to Huntley and Avyanna

29
BROOKE WYCKOFF

Brooke Wyckoff is a Seminole through and through. She started her career at Florida State as an All-American basketball player and then after nine years in the WNBA became an assistant coach and eventually the head coach of the women's team at her alma mater. Coaching and motherhood sharpened many of the athletic skills that Wyckoff already possessed and it also reinforced her belief in the power of the team. That network of support has always been important to Wyckoff and especially so during two defining periods in her life—when the single mom announced her pregnancy in 2013 and 10 years later when she was diagnosed with breast cancer. Wyckoff smiles and radiates true gratitude and joy even through the challenges she has faced. This is who she is. This is why she's an incredible leader for her players and a strong, tough mother to her daughter Avery, who will add her own perspective at the end of this chapter.

"When I initially received my cancer diagnosis, my biggest fear was: is my child going to have her mother? She was nine and she didn't even know what breast cancer was. I didn't really know how to—or want to—explain it to her because it's scary. I didn't tell her anything until I knew what was going to happen, and luckily it was, 'I'm going to be okay.' I started chemo the day after Christmas and finished the last day of February. It was like a two-month process, and I feel so blessed. Some people have tons of treatments, and I only had four—one every three weeks. I didn't have the most drastic type of chemotherapy, the kind that totally wrecks you, and now there is some ongoing treatment that I have to do but nothing like the chemo.

I saw Brooke during that basketball season that she was diagnosed with cancer, and though she still smiled and sashayed around on the sidelines (dressed to the nines in heels, mind you), I know the cancer took its toll. Initially, she only confided in Jose "Esmo" Ramon Esmoris, her husband since 2022. She had surgery to remove a cancerous tumor in October of 2023, only then revealing the severity of her situation to her team and to those outside her inner circle. She did not miss a game even when clumps of her hair started falling out during timeouts. She shaved her head and covered it with a wig. Brooke never stopped being there for her players, but she also acknowledges the importance of the people who stood by her side and supported her along the way.

—*J.H.*

"Through any adversity, any hard things in life, there are those silver linings that come out of them. Things like this deepen your marriage, deepen your relationship, show you the meaning of true love that you committed to when everything was still like puppy love. This is what we were really saying when we said our vows. The way my husband is acting and taking care of me and truly loving me, this is what it is. Those moments dawn on you in regular life, but when something like this comes up, you really see who you're with. He was a rock, just positive, caring, nurturing, patient, concerned, the right mix of all those things. And then also [former Florida State head coach] Sue Semrau was there for me, asking me, 'How are you? Tell me the hard things. Tell me what it's really like.' The questions nobody else really knew how to ask, she was asking. Sue was at every chemo treatment that I had, and it hit me later on that this coach/player relationship is almost like a parent/child relationship. She is still caring for me as one of her players even so many years later. She's my mentor, my former coach, my daughter's godmother, just an incredible human being. When I got pregnant with Avery in 2013, Sue was asking me a lot of questions then, too, like, 'What's this going to look like? What do we need? How can we help you?' I said, 'I don't know.' I really had no idea. She was worried about things like postpartum depression, stress, childcare.

"So that got me thinking. I realized two things: A, how grateful I was for the advice but also B, how much help I needed. There is no way you can do this without a good support group, whether you're married or not. If you want to have a career as a mother, you have to have that. I was blessed to have a boss that didn't flinch when I told her I was pregnant, even though I was a single mom at the time. When I was about five months pregnant, I was out recruiting, and my belly was getting harder and harder to ignore or hide. Word started to spread that I was expecting, and slowly other coaches, who were moms, started seeking me out. The things they were telling me—their struggles, their stories, their advice—were so encouraging. I was like, 'Wow, this is cool. Give me more!'

"And back then only about 10 percent of Division I NCAA women's basketball coaches were mothers. So there weren't a lot of us out there, but I felt this pull to find them and to try and bring us all together. I met Erika Lambert, a woman who had temporarily stepped away from coaching to raise her two small children. She and I talked, had a great connection, and decided in 2014 to start our own team: Moms in Coaching. We have an annual meeting at the NCAA women's Final Four where we provide a space for women to connect and support one another as we go through this crazy journey of motherhood.

"Being a single mom with a young kid is just…hard. Being a single mom at any point is difficult, but with a baby that is completely dependent on you, there were so many moments where I just felt like I was treading water. That's the best way that I can put it. The physical feeling of just having so much to do between your child and your work in one day, you have this long list of things that need to be done, you need to be in two places at once, and you're dead tired. In those moments I always go back to our Moms in Coaching meetings. I think about conversations that I've had, where I know I am not the only one doing this, not the only one feeling this, that it's gonna be okay. I'm going to get the work done. I'm going to be there for my child. Being able to say, 'I'm not alone' has been huge for me, and that's definitely because of Moms in Coaching and I think because of my background as an athlete.

"We as women are fighters. For me as a female athlete, I always had this chip on my shoulder of: *This is who I am. I can be a professional basketball player.* Then, when it came time to be a mother, I still had that chip, that feeling of wanting to go out and prove that we, as women, yeah, we can do this, too! We can be these great athletes, be successful in our careers, be mothers, hold it all together in a world that doesn't value women as much in general. That definitely carries over into being a mother and balancing all of it. Growing up as a female athlete, I was very familiar with that feeling of having something to prove. I also had—I don't know exactly what to call it—but I had that dig deep factor, the ability to push past the limit of what you think you're capable of. Working hard, knowing what physical pain feels like and pushing through that, knowing what disappointment feels like left and right, and having to get back up and fight through, that's all so valuable as a parent. When you're exhausted in a practice or a game and you're like, 'I don't know if I can go anymore' and then you do, that's how we all have felt as mothers. I push myself and demand success. Even when I was pregnant, I thought, *I've run all these lines and done suicides* [sprinting drills], *I've had two ACL surgeries. How hard could labor be?* I know, I know, I was way too cocky. I was wrong about that. It was the hardest thing I've ever done. But I just had this mentality of: *I've got this.*

"It's funny. At first I wanted everybody to tell me what to do. Tell me what it would be like. Give me the manual. But, of course, that's not how it works. Nobody can really tell you anything for sure about work and motherhood. It's a journey and it all comes down to you, who you need to be, what you are feeling in the moment. I think in talking with other women it has helped me to just see that—even if I can't see it in the moment—it's going to be okay. Your kid is going to be okay and so are you.

"For me it did not work to mix. I was not as good of a coach and I was not as good of a mother when I had my baby on the road with me. I wasn't good at it. Some people are. I wanted my child to be well taken care of and in her routine even if I wasn't there and I wanted to be able to fully focus on work when I was on the road. But that took me a few years to realize. Avery is a little older now, and I make sure I'm very clear with her as to the why behind what we're doing. It's being intentional and saying, 'I have to go do this because this is my job. You go to the school you go to, and you live in the house you live in, and you get to do the things you want to do because Mommy has this job.' I want to make sure she sees all the positives—not just the material things—but the fact that she gets to go on these trips with our team and be around these awesome players, and all these things she gets to do because I do this job. And me doing this job means I have to go on the road and be away sometimes. That's real life.

"And you know what? I can do this job just as well, if not better, after having a child. Being a mom has made me a better coach. When I look at it that way and remind myself that it's the truth even if it doesn't always feel like it, I think, *Yes, I can handle this.* I think you do see more mothers who are coaches now, too. It's a byproduct of this explosion of exposure we're seeing with women's basketball. Those of us who are in the game already know how amazing it is, but now the general public is getting to see that it's okay to watch women's basketball and it's okay to be a mom that coaches. It feels more accepted and encouraged and empowered, but women are still craving that support. When you see moms like Adia Barnes Coppa breastfeeding at halftime of the national championship game, moments like that are so cool. It's like, *I'm not crazy!* Or at least if I am, it's not just me."

My mom is a Tough Mother because she gets through problems she has at work and at home and she takes care of me at the same time. She is such an awesome mom! She is also a Tough Mother because she doesn't let cancer stop her from doing what she loves to do.

I'd like to tell my mom that I love everything she does for me. She is so loving and kind, and that's why she's the best mom in the world! I recently discovered that I would like to be an entrepreneur when I grow up. I also want to be a mom someday. I want to have kids that make the world a better place, and it will be fun taking care of them.

—*daughter Avery at age 10*

30
SUSAN SAINT JAMES
EBERSOL

AP Images

This Emmy Award-winning actress is married to Dick Ebersol, the man who arguably transformed the business of sports television when he ran the division called NBC Sports and Olympics. Susan Saint James Ebersol is best known for her roles as Rock Hudson's wife in TV's McMillan & Wife *and Kate McArdle in the hit series* Kate & Allie. *But she retired early to spend more time with her family. Giving of herself and supporting others is just who Susan is. Even in her darkest hours after losing her youngest son in a plane crash, Susan found comfort in reaching out to other parents who lost a child and offering them her support.*

If you were to ask her about her career, she'd probably manage to shift the conversation to her children and grandchildren or she'd tell you about some of the sporting events she traveled to with her husband. It was at those events that she'd often check in on many of the women who worked at NBC to see how they were managing the challenges of family and career and in the process she'd share some really cool stories about how she handled it back in the day.

When Susan became a mom in the early 1970s, she did the juggle when it wasn't all that common. And being a public figure, she showed those of us who were watching that it was possible to have both a career and a family. She even brazenly breastfed one of her kids on national television.

You can't help but smile and laugh along when you hear Susan's voice, one that is unique and endearing—with an edge—in its raspiness. To schmooze with Susan is to feel joy. She jumps from one hot topic to another while keeping you entertained and often empowered along the way. Her world is peppered with all kinds of interesting people and places. And wherever she has been, Susan has helped to create a culture that validates the challenges of working moms.

"My dad told me one time, 'You have a great voice. You should be a receptionist in a law firm. They would love that voice.' I remember thinking, *That's ridiculous, I'll be a lawyer!* I just already had this confidence, I think, because it felt like so much was changing around that time. I remember reading *Glamour* magazine in high school and I saw this article by Gloria Steinem, where she said, 'Go to the beach this summer. Have an affair!' I thought that was so radical.

"I never thought of not having kids because I worked. I never thought of it. My mom was a teacher, but she stopped working by the time that I came along. You know in those days, it was like, 'Oh, you work?' That was more the exception than it was the rule. When I came home from school, she was always on the couch with the newspaper over her face. I'd say, 'Mom, what are you doing?' And she'd say, 'Planning dinner.' And to the end of her life, when she was 95, I could call her up and she would always answer. I had that kind of mom. But I remember thinking that I was going to be an actress. I was going to do plays *and* be a mom. I wanted to have it all. I said to myself, *How hard could it be? And why doesn't my mom do that?* I didn't tell her that, but that's what I thought. She was beautiful and smart, but she wasn't given that self-confidence then to be able to do so much more. Plus, I always wanted to make my own money.

"When I started my career, I worked on the movie *Where Angels Go Trouble Follows!* I saw actress Rosalind Russell had a maid with her. And I say 'maid' because this woman only took care of Rosalind's needs—not hair, not makeup—she just took care of her on set. She also worked for Natalie Wood, who was one of my favorites. So I thought, *Maybe if I get famous, I'll have someone on set who can take care of me and then I can have my kids with me.* And I actually had the same woman when I had my first child. I think she was like 100 by then. But I was like, *Yes, I've made it!*

"I had no squabbles about breastfeeding either. I was a hippie. I'd pull my boob out; it didn't bother me. I went to the La Leche League, a very small group started in Chicago by a bunch of midwestern housewives, in 1971. These women still wanted to be who they were, but they also wanted to be able to sit on a park bench and nurse their kids. They were radicals, but they didn't look like radicals. I loved what they were all about, so I went and spoke at their convention. It was the beginning of that movement. I was in *People* magazine, and my son Harmony was on my lap, and I said that he was still nursing at the age of two. I got hate mail from people. I went on *The Tonight Show* and would tell Johnny Carson that I was nursing, and he'd say, 'Oh, no, I don't want to know about that!' It was a whole new world.

"The one thing about being an actress is there aren't many days off. When you're not filming, you're out promoting or doing something else. There are big breaks, though. I would get like three straight months where I was home and I could be a full-time mom and then I could go back to working. But it really gets tough if you have to go on location. When the kids are babies, it's easier, but once they're in school, you can't have the kids on set every day. It's like half mother/half actress, and you just can't do that. I might bring them for a weekend if it was a fun project but never a movie that would be scary or intense. When I was working on the TV series *Kate & Allie*, I had to work in New York City, and we lived in Connecticut, which was a two-hour drive. I'd go down on a Monday morning, finish taping on Thursday, then go home. I didn't want my work to disrupt my kids' lives, so they stayed in Connecticut with my mom and dad, who helped to oversee everything.

"You have to ditch so many expectations about who you are and how you are when you're a working mom. It's so different today from when I was working, and there was no Internet, nobody outside your door. It's so intrusive now. I look at these women, who every time they walk out of their apartment or their house, they're in a completely coordinated outfit, their hair is done, and they're just going to Starbucks. I couldn't have done that. That's really hard, especially with a family.

"My generation, when I was in seventh and eighth grade, it was like we don't have girlfriends. We only have boyfriends. We dismissed the idea of needing girlfriends. But I've always been a little different in that I do appreciate the ways that women can support one another. If there is competition or conflict, I try to get out in front of it and be supportive instead, kind of like Beyoncé and Taylor Swift. Everyone wants them to be competitive, but they went to each other's concerts and film premieres. And when Taylor started going to the Kansas City Chiefs games, she immediately made friends with the quarterback's wife [Brittany Mahomes]. One time early in my career, I was under contract with one of the studios and I was up for a movie. This director came along and told me the role was mine. Then I was watching TV one day and saw that someone else got the role. I was brokenhearted. I thought, *How could they do that?* I was so jealous and mad. And then one day I heard this voice on the beach near where I lived—I had this ratty, little house in Malibu where I had to broom the mice out every day—and it was the girl who got the role that was supposed to be mine. So I went out there and said, 'We should be friends.' I wanted to clear the air. I thought, *I can't have this tension between us.* That whole experience turned out to be really empowering for me. She and I did become friends, and I had no more competition with her. I was just rooting for her all the time.

Okay, full disclosure here: Dick Ebersol, Susan's husband, was my boss for many years, and I was one of the lucky working moms who Susan checked in on at NBC.

She gave me many parenting pointers over the years, but maybe the most impactful one was to trust the connection between a mother and her baby. So when Susan invited me and my newborn daughter to lunch at a fancy NYC restaurant and Claire needed to be fed, Susan encouraged me to breastfeed right at the table. This was 1996, and you didn't see that much, if at all. But since she was the boss' wife, I figured I had no choice but to oblige, right? So just like that, I pulled out my (sorry, kids, I'm going to say it)...um...boob...and fed my baby. With Susan as an advocate and a voice in her husband's ear, I believe she made him a more supportive boss to many of us working mamas.

—*A.L.*

"I remember talking to Dick about Aimee before she started working for him in sports and the fact that she was a mom of a young son. It was a really busy time at NBC—getting all new properties, traveling to big events—but I always saw Aimee as a whole person, not just the job. When we traveled with Dick, I brought the kids a lot. I always liked when people brought their families to work events because we all got to know each other so much better, but there were times, too, when we had to leave the kids at home. And the whole thing about leaving your kids and worrying about how they're going to do without you can be exaggerated. I remember when my son Teddy was going to go to boarding school. It was close to home. When he first started, Dick and I went to one of the NBC golf tournaments, and I couldn't be reached. Teddy called several times and when I saw the messages—'I don't want to stay here. Why aren't you answering me?'—it was about 10 different things he talked through that eventually led to 'Never mind, I'm fine.' He worked it out. My mother used to say that about me, too: 'I don't worry about you. You'll run any problem through your mind and figure it out.' Well, that's what we do as mothers."

31
SASCHA MAYER
AND KATE TORGERSEN

Sascha Mayer

Kate Torgersen

Two women—Mamava chief experience officer and co-founder Sascha Mayer and Milk Stork chief executive officer and founder Kate Torgersen—have helped revolutionize the experience of breastfeeding for working moms on the go. Mayer's Mamava is responsible for the pod-like lactation suites that you have probably seen (and used) in airports and sporting venues. Through her own experiences as a working mom, Mayer saw a need and worked to create a solution that would help and support all mothers.

"I have always believed in the power of design to solve problems. In the case of Mamava, I wasn't able to ease my own breastfeeding issues, but I did see an opportunity to help others.

"My kids, Cal and Storey, were born in 2003 and 2006, respectively. I was a working mother and I breastfed both of them, even while traveling. That meant all of the usual difficulties—finding a place to pump, figuring out how to tell my co-workers and clients that I needed time to pump, storing and transporting the milk, and experiencing the awkwardness that came along with it all. Usually stuck pumping in a bathroom somewhere, I felt demoralized, undignified, and so, so alone. Those were the words that I used in my TED Talk in 2019 because it all felt to me like an almost invisible problem. If you weren't in the thick of it, you had no idea. And once women had gone through it and survived, they packed up their pumps and moved on. But the problem remained. That's a bit of why I stuck with it.

"Breastfeeding is like a third job. You have your family and your household to take care of, you have your career, and then you have the job of breastfeeding. And breastfeeding requires many dedicated hours to do it with the pump and the nursing and all of the equipment. But when my babies came along, there was really no infrastructure in place to help me deal with it. As a design professional, I saw an opportunity to solve a problem that was literally right under my nose. I believed that through innovation and design we could not only tackle this problem, but also shift people's thinking and start a conversation.

"So then my third child, Mamava, was born. My colleague and fellow mother, Christine Dodson, and I launched the company and placed our first free-standing lactation suite in the Burlington [Vermont] airport in 2013. I think there were a lot of forces at play that encouraged us to give it a shot. There were our own experiences, of course, but there also seemed to be an uptick in breastfeeding in general. Women were leaning into their own needs, asserting themselves, and they needed to be supported. Our lactation suites have changed some over the years, but their distinctive pod-like shape makes them hard to miss. We did that on purpose. There's something really powerful about how our pods stand out. They spark conversation about breastfeeding, which is a good thing, and maybe even help encourage more women to want to breastfeed.

"On the inside of every unit—and this has been the case since our very first one—we have a mirror with the words, 'Looking Good, Mama.' On the one hand, it's practical, right? You're disrobing and how many times when you button back up do you discover that you have the buttons wrong? You need to be able to see yourself and get ready for the next part of your day. But it's also about having the conversation, letting that mother know that she's being seen in this important phase of her life. *We see you. And we support you.* [Authors' note: Mamava has retained this powerful message over the years, even though some newer pods have dropped the "Mama" at the end of "Looking Good."] I think mothers have an incredible energy. I see moms as this driving force that can be just amazing. You need to harness that power, and at Mamava we want to do all that we can to facilitate it. We are always keeping an eye on—and pushing for—legislation to better protect the rights of breastfeeding moms. And we believe that breastfeeding should no longer be the invisible problem that I felt it was in my days as a new mom."

* * *

Like Mayer, Kate Torgersen saw a need and worked to create a solution that would help and support all mothers. Milk Stork helps moms ship their breast milk safely and securely. In August of 2015, Torgersen officially launched Milk Stork. Since then she has set the gold standard for breast milk shipping logistics. As of 2024 more than 850 companies offered Milk Stork as an employee benefit, and Milk Stork has safely shipped more than 3.2 million ounces of breast milk.

"As a kid I did ice skating, gymnastics, ballet, soccer, softball, basketball, tennis. I wound up playing NCAA Division I soccer at Cal—I was a goalkeeper—and then I was a pro ski instructor and a firefighter. I firmly believe that how I approach things is 100 percent driven from my experience in sports. It's how I approached—survived?—the early years of motherhood and how I launched my business, Milk Stork. My husband and I had our first son, Jax, in 2010 followed by our twins, Finn and Zoë, in 2013. I was a working mom, but the kind of work that I did changed drastically once I got a real taste of just how doggone hard it was.

"With Jax I always tell people that it was rainbows and unicorns breastfeeding him. He had the perfect latch, he breastfed for 18 months, and I never worried that he had enough milk. It was a dream. I'll admit that with the twins I went in overconfident. I took a lactation class for twins specifically and, boy, did I need it. It was unreal. I had two different breastfeeding relationships at the same time. Different body types, different circadian rhythms, appetites, sleep schedules, everything. One could latch; one couldn't. One only wanted one side; the other would go to both. Even onboarding and offboarding them when they had their wiggly heads, holding them at the same time, was incredibly challenging.

"I had a business trip and I didn't know how to do any of this, but I knew I didn't want to throw in the towel. We had fought so hard, but the sheer logistics were overwhelming. The twins were consuming a gallon of milk every two days. I know; it's insane. So on a four-day trip, I needed to figure out how to handle production of two gallons of milk on the road, keep it safe, keep it fresh, and get it back home. I was working at CLIF Bar at the time and I'm sure they would have been happy to accommodate me and let me not take the trip. But professionally I was all in. I wanted to go. So I did it. I pumped every three hours on the dot—middle of the night, too. I didn't want to have 10,000 little baggies of milk. So I bought some Nalgene water bottles and started filling those up. I had my suitcase, my computer bag, and a cooler bag holding four Ziploc gallon-sized bags of ice and two gallons of milk, which probably weighed like 25 pounds. I was in the airport, heading home, and I got asked by a dude why I had so much breast milk, why it was in Nalgene bottles instead of bags. Ugh! I had to dump my ice when it started melting and go get fresh ice from some bartender in the airport terminal. I got home and said, 'That sucked.'

"The next day I called my dad, and said, 'I have this idea.' I wanted to create a way for moms to get their breast milk home safely. Business travel is one of the hardest things because it intensifies the logistics of everything not to mention breastfeeding around the clock while you're away. Not only are you separated from your child, but you're also on this insane, every three-hour pumping schedule typically in a demoralizing or degrading place, not getting the respect for the job you're doing. I felt there had to be a better way. So I created one. With Milk Stork I'm providing a logistical solution for an emotionally taxing issue. Let us help get the milk home. It's one less burden for working mothers to bear. I hate that so many women feel forced into a choice that they shouldn't have to make; they feel so beaten down by working and traveling and breastfeeding that they give up on it much sooner than they otherwise would. These are the things that motivated me—when I was hooked up to my own breast pump—to create Milk Stork. Is leaving and pumping still going to be emotionally difficult? Of course! But let's try and make some aspects of it a little bit easier, maybe educate some people along the way, too. Pumping is such a mysterious event to employers. There is a lot of Breastfeeding 101 that goes on. I feel no shame, though, in explaining this to people. I feel righteous! Breastfeeding is part of the human experience. I refuse to feel any shame in explaining or talking about it.

"And you know what I discovered, too? This amazing sisterhood. I launched Milk Stork direct-to-consumer because I didn't think I could convince companies to do it. But the moms would use it. Then they would ask their company to offer it as a benefit to themselves and other moms. They would make connections with other women in the company, and those connections are so vital. I'm still in a Facebook group on breastfeeding. There's this community that carries forward once you've gone through the gauntlet. These are my people. It's similar, really, to that feeling of being on a team."

Fond Farewell

Now, the hard part—saying goodbye. We could start singing Boyz II Men, "It's so hard…to say goodbye…to yesterday." But instead—you're welcome—we'll just sign off in our own way. We promised to create a sisterhood filled with fellow Tough Mothers who would share their stories with you, sisters who would be honest and vulnerable and who would be right there with you as you try to manage your way through your own juggle struggle, sisters who know that this working mother life can be really, really hard. And like most things, it's a whole lot easier when you can go through it in good company. We hope you've been able to find that here.

We all have these moments where we feel straight shot down by motherhood. As you continue your own journey, experience your own struggles, stress, emotions, and exhaustion, we hope you'll remember that you always have a place on our team. We hope you feel stronger and more supported. We hope you realize that you are, in fact, tough…as a mother. You are strong even in the moments you feel weak. You are tough even through the most trying of times. You are exactly the mother that your children need you to be.

Depending on the age of your children, you may not be able to look to them for any kind of validation right now, so we wanted to share what our kids had to say. They made us laugh, cry, and, yes, feel pretty damn good! And we know your kids are just waiting to tell you what a wonderful job you are doing. So keep this book handy because…well…life changes, and our hope is that you can come back to our sisterhood and pick up the book whenever you need it. And that each time you do, you are reminded that we are all here rooting for you. Your fellow Tough Mothers will always have your back.

I always knew my mom was different. She worked. So she wasn't there for school pick-up, and we had nannies. But looking back, I think that made me stronger, a lot more resilient and self-sufficient. Seeing her and what she's done has given me an inherent respect for women that I take into the world now. That didn't need to be taught; it was just ingrained. I remember thinking of her as an authority figure, then more of a confidante, a peer, a friend and a support system. She's a boss. She's impressive, silly, and funny. She's definitely a tough mother.

—*Aimee's son Jay at age 32*

My mom's quick-witted, unconventional, unapologetic, professional, and classy. She's a very classy lady. I don't feel like there's a cap to what I can achieve because I saw her working and being successful from a very young age. Not having her home all the time taught me to appreciate the time we had together and the memories we made growing up. And now as a I make my own way in the working world, I'm able to come to her for guidance that's incredibly helpful. I want to be a working mom; I don't want to be put in a box. Financial independence is important to me. But there is one thing that really pissed me off growing up and still does to this day. She doesn't always answer her phone! Jay and I are notorious for repeatedly calling our mother.

—*Aimee's daughter Claire at age 27*

Even when my mom has to go away for work, she still makes it good for us. She likes her job and she makes us happy even if she's not there. Through every trip, every place she's gone, she did it perfectly. No matter how she did it, it's all come back together in an amazing way. You can't really get better than that.

—*Jenn's daughter Madison at age 13*

My mom is the definition of devotion. Although she does spend a lot of time preparing for her games and traveling for work, she will always put her family first and make time to spend with us. I can tell she really loves what she does and I look up to her for it. The times when my mom left for work were a lot harder when I was little. *Where was she going? Why was she leaving?* Now that I'm older, I have a better understanding of her work, and it doesn't bother me. Seeing her be happy with her job makes me happy. My mom is truly tough...as a mother. I don't think people really understand what it means to be a mom, including me, but I think my mom has done an amazing job raising me and my sister. I would describe her as strong, powerful, moving, loving, compassionate, and...practically perfect in every way. (I had to get a Mary Poppins reference in there.) I couldn't ask for anyone better. I would like to tell her that she is the best mom that I could ask for, and she doesn't always need to feel like she has to do better—because she is already perfect.

—Jenn's daughter Ashley at age 17

Acknowledgments

We would like to thank everyone who supported this dream of ours. First, to all of the amazing moms who allowed us to interview them and share their stories with you, thank you. You are incredible and inspiring, generous with time that we know you don't have, and true embodiments of what it means to be a Tough Mother. Thank you for showing us that we aren't alone! And to everyone who helped connect us to our Tough Mothers, including:

Dan Levy at Wasserman
Claire McCarthy at Angel City FC
John Hricay at HAWI Management
Ann Pechaver at Mamava
Shelby Stanger
Debbie Phelps
Aloni Ford
Kate Scott
Brett Goodman
Jacob Ullman
Tim Scanlan
Cristianna Vazquez at Ally

To Julie Foudy, we are so very grateful for your support and for being a part of this book. You are the fucking best.

We'd like to give an anonymous shout-out to those moms who weren't comfortable being interviewed because they didn't feel supported along their journey. We hope we can in some way help move the needle by showing how critical support and sisterhood are in this often messy balance we strive for.

Thank you to our incredible agent Sandy Montag for believing in this project and to his team, especially Jill Driban, Luca Giacobbe, Alanna Frisby Hernandez for their support throughout this process.

Thanks to the team at Triumph particularly Bill Ames, Michelle Bruton, and Jeff Fedotin.

To David Hildreth, our talented cover artist (and Jenn's awesome brother), thank you for translating our collective visions into one kick ass book cover.

To David Hirshey and Roger Director, thank you for your input and guidance.

* * *

It's hard not to get emotional as I think about all of the people who have helped make this beautiful dream a reality. To my husband, Chris, thank you for believing in me and for understanding when I had yet another project to pull me away from you and our girls. You have always been there holding things down, and I couldn't do this, any of this, without you. To steal a line from *The Avengers: Endgame* that the girls like to use, "I love you 3,000." To my daughters, Ashley and Madison, who would comfort *me* when I apologized and agonized over all the time I was devoting to this book, thank you. You knew it would be worth it, even though it sacrificed more of our time together, and I am in awe of the two incredible women you are growing up to be. You made me a mother and you make me proud every day. I am overwhelmed with love and gratitude for you both.

To my mom, Sandra Hildreth, my original Tough Mother, you are everything that I have ever wanted to be as a mother. Thank you for setting the greatest example and for giving me the gift of your love and support.

To my dad, Joe Hildreth, I would not be who I am without you. Thank you. I love you.

To my friends who read sample chapters (book club shoutout to Margo Bryk, Victoria Woodison, Kristine Honey, Sherri Palmer, Elisabeth Madden, Kate Jackson, Kristin Kohrman, Michelle Wilde, and Jill Konrad) and my co-workers who continued to encourage me throughout this process, thank you. I cherish all of you and I needed that support through all of the ups and downs and rejections and re-writes.

To Rhea Lyons, who took a chance on me, thank you. You believed in this book when no one else did.

To Laura Hopper, thank you for being so gracious with your time and editorial advice early in the process.

To all of the women that inspire me every day, I see you. All of the coaches and broadcasters and athletes who are hustling and juggling work life and mom life, I appreciate every one of you.

And to Aimee, the missing piece of the puzzle, the Queen of Connections, my partner in curly-haired crime, we did it. Thank you for being you, for believing that we could combine our two ideas and turn it into something special and for making this happen.

—*J.H.*

* * *

First and foremost, thank you to my family (in order of appearance)—my parents, Norma Dianne and Eli Bauer, who have given me love and encouragement through every chapter of my story. My sister and cheerleader, Laura, for being my very best friend... always. To my husband Wayne. It's been one hell of a ride so far, and you've been there to support and love me every step of the way. And to our two incredible children, Jay and Claire, who are my reason for everything.

During this working mom life, I have been fortunate enough to have the most incredible bosses, who have helped make me better, personally and professionally, and for that I cannot thank you enough—Lou Del Prete, Tory Street, Dick Ebersol, Sandy Montag, Eric Shanks, and Mark Silverman.

Thank you to two brilliant writers who believed in this project from the beginning and gave me the confidence to get out of my comfort zone—Jim Miller and Seth Davis. And to those who doubted me (who shall remain nameless), you fueled the fire more than you will ever know.

And to my friends and "sisters" Mary-Hollis Beighly, Debi Conocenti, Sharon Chang, Susan Ebersol, Randy Frank, Sue Giella, Judy Goldstein, Kate Hogan, Lisa Lax, Caroline Leone, Doreen Lockwood, Jill Montgomery, Laura Olsziewski, Betty Olt, Babette Perry, Linda Richmand, Vicki Rosen, Sue Stogel, Debbie Tonelli, Melissa Baron Weiss, Denise White, Alicia Ybarbo, your support, belief and encouragement mean the world to me.

To fellow Triumphers, Kenny Albert, Amy Trask, and Ric Bucher.

And finally, to Jenn Hildreth—it has been an honor and a blast traveling down this road with you. We learned, we grew, we laughed, and I almost cried...and WE DID IT!

—*A.L.*

Sources

Books

Good Inside: A Guide to Becoming the Parent You Want to Be
Together: The Healing Power of Human Connection in a Sometimes Lonely World

Periodicals

Fast Company
Forbes
Los Angeles Times

Websites

Adweek.com
Brainyquotes.com
Clevelandclinic.org
ESPN.com
Essentiallysports.com
FIFPRO.org
Heavy.com
Hilaryphelps.com
Kabri.uk
Psychologytoday.com
Reachupincorporated.org
Womenssportsfoundation.org

Audio

Your Mom, podcast episode No. 59: "Super Bowl series: Dr. Christina Mack on the science of sports, mom guilt, and female friendships"

TED Talk by Brené Brown: "Listening to Shame"